经典篇章阅读与欣赏

车向前 张 颖 冯 羽 编著

西北工业大学出版社

西安

【内容简介】 本书着眼于人类历史上与文学、语言、社会、人生等相关的经典篇章,选取其中富含意蕴的原文进行阅读、理解、欣赏,共设计10个章节,包括神话篇、社会篇、自然篇、教育篇、诗歌篇、修辞篇、爱情篇、家庭篇、游记篇、哲思篇等。每章节的结构包括导语、经典篇章3篇与注解与练习题。教材结构设计合理,经典篇章体裁多样,并配有作者与作品的背景介绍、英文释义与注释,最大程度地照顾各个水平的读者群体,方便读者进行阅读与欣赏;各类练习题的设置充分注重对学生英语基本能力的培养,以加强学生对所选文本大意的理解,同时激发阅读兴趣,培养学生的人文情怀。

本书既可作为高校公共英语经典阅读通识类课程的教材,也适合英语专业学生和对经典文献感兴趣且有一定英文基础的读者阅读、参考。

图书在版编目(CIP)数据

经典篇章选读与欣赏/车向前,张颖,冯羽编著
.— 西安:西北工业大学出版社,2022.12
ISBN 978-7-5612-8536-7

Ⅰ.①经… Ⅱ.①车… ②张… ③冯… Ⅲ.①英语-阅读教学-高等学校-教材 Ⅳ.①H319.37

中国版本图书馆CIP数据核字(2022)第224461号

JINGDIAN PIANZHANG YUEDU YU XINSHANG
经 典 篇 章 阅 读 与 欣 赏
车向前 张 颖 冯 羽 编著

责任编辑:杨 军 张 炜	策划编辑:张 炜
责任校对:隋秀娟	装帧设计:董晓伟

出版发行:西北工业大学出版社
通信地址:西安市友谊西路127号　　　邮编:710072
电　　话:(029)88491757,88493844
网　　址:www.nwpup.com
印 刷 者:陕西向阳印务有限公司
开　　本:787 mm×1 092 mm　　　1/16
印　　张:10.5
字　　数:276千字
版　　次:2022年12月第1版　　　2022年12月第1次印刷
书　　号:ISBN 978-7-5612-8536-7
定　　价:49.00元

如有印装问题请与出版社联系调换

前　言

　　身处于信息爆炸的时代,伴随着媒介的高速发展,经典阅读的意义与价值更需要被挖掘、被认知,因为经典阅读能够帮助我们在追寻世界的原始图景中,更好地处理日常世界和价值世界的关系。在全球化的今日世界,经典阅读可以帮助我们回溯自身传统并培育国际视野,由此提升洞察和理解世界的能力。青年学子阅读经典,其意义不仅在于汇聚广博知识、增强语言能力,更在于使用语言文字去思考万物本质、精神内核,在仔细研读和格物致知中端正品行、加强修养,在理解他者中观照自身、开阔视野。

　　与此同时,随着我国"一带一路"、人类命运共同体和中国文化"走出去"等倡议和战略的深入实施,外语教育改革和人才培养进入了新时期,其核心任务已经从发挥语言的知识工具性作用,转变为更加注重不同语言背后的价值内涵。基于此,需要编撰教材进一步挖掘经典篇章中的人文内涵,把中华优秀文化传播结合到教材建设当中。围绕人类历史上的经典篇章展开教学,能够在提升学生语言能力与水平的同时,提高学生的人文素养,使他们更好地认识历史经典精要,养成阅读意识、思考意识,清楚地认识世界文化发展的统一性和多样性,树立本民族文化自觉与文化自信。

　　本书以立德树人思想为根本指导,旨在帮助读者,特别是帮助学生树立正确的思想观念,在锻炼其基本语言能力的同时,启发其将阅读与思考、阅读与拓展视野紧密结合。本书着眼于人类历史上与文学、语言、社会、教育、人生等相关的经典篇章,选取其中富含意蕴与内涵的篇章进行阅读、欣赏、理解,共设计 10 个章节,包括神话篇、社会篇、自然篇、教育篇、诗歌篇、修辞篇、爱情篇、家庭篇、游记篇、哲思篇等,选取了《山海经》《道德经》《诗经》《孝经》《文心雕龙》等中国经典思想巨著,也包括《师说》《桃花源记》《前赤壁赋》《天台山游记》等美文,外文经典名篇则选取了《荷马史诗》《修辞学》《瓦尔登湖》等。每章节的结构包括导语、经典篇章 3 篇及练习。导语:对经典篇章作者与作品背景进行介绍。经典篇章 3 篇:形式多样,既有中文经典,又有英文经典,均配有详尽的英文释义与注释,方便学生阅读欣赏,并提供一篇相关扩展阅读文献。练习:包括单选题、判断题、翻译题、讨论题等题型,最大程度地照顾各个水平的读者群体,同时注重对学生英语阅读、写作、翻译等各个基本能力的培养,以加强学生对所选文本大意的理解,同时激发学生的阅读兴趣,培养其人文情怀。

　　本书的特点还体现在内容多元、话题丰富、释义详尽。本书介绍了经典文献在文学、语言、艺术、教育等方面的特色,同时凸显中国元素,重视中国传统文化的介绍与学习,引导学生讲好中国故事;突破单一话题,充分关注到神话、社会、修辞、旅游等篇章内容,同时每章节 3 篇文献均相互关联,特色突出;在重视经典文献概要介绍的同时,充分重视对内容的理解,从词语、句子、段落、篇章等各个层面对原文进行详细释疑,最大程度地帮助学生准确理解原文。

本书由西北工业大学外国语学院车向前、重庆邮电大学外国语学院张颖、西安理工大学人文与外国语学院冯羽编写。其中车向前负责第2、4、6、10章节,张颖负责第3、5、9章节,冯羽负责第1、7、8章节。

本书受西北工业大学2022年教材建设项目与教育部首批新文科建设项目"西部国防院校跨学科交叉融合型英语一流专业建设新模式研究"(课题编号:22GZ13131)资助,在此谨表诚挚感谢。

在编写过程中,笔者借鉴、参阅了相关文献、资料,在此对其作者表达深深的谢意。

由于笔者水平与经验有限,书中难免存在不足之处,请广大读者批评指正。

编者

2022年5月

Contents

Unit One Mythology 1

    Session One　The Classic of Mountains and Seas 2

    Session Two　Iliad 5

    Session Three (Extensive Reading)　Theogony 14

Unit Two Society 17

    Session One　The Peach Blossom Spring 18

    Session Two　The Social Contract 21

    Session Three (Extensive Reading)　A Modest Proposal 31

Unit Three Nature 35

    Session One　The First Ode to the Red Cliff 36

    Session Two　Walden 38

    Session Three (Extensive Reading)　Nature 50

Unit Four Education 52

    Session One　On the Teacher 53

    Session Two　Emile 56

    Session Three (Extensive Reading)　On Education 66

Unit Five Poetry 70

    Session One　"The Great Preface" to the Book of Songs 71

    Session Two　Preface to Lyrical Ballads 75

    Session Three (Extensive Reading)　Min Shi 83

Unit Six Rhetoric 84

    Session One　Dragon-Carving and Literary Mind 85

    Session Two　Rhetoric 88

    Session Three (Extensive Reading)　Institutio Oratoria 96

Unit Seven　Love ··· 99

　Session One　Book of Poetry ·· 100
　Session Two　Sonnets ·· 104
　Session Three (Extensive Reading)　Of Love ·· 111

Unit Eight　Family ··· 113

　Session One　The Book of Filial Piety ·· 114
　Session Two　On Family ·· 116
　Session Three (Extensive Reading)　Ten Lectures on Cognitive Linguistics ······· 123

Unit Nine　Travel ··· 126

　Session One　Terrace of Heaven Mountain ·· 127
　Session Two　Recollections of a Tour Made in Scotland ································· 133
　Session Three (Extensive Reading)　The Sketch Book of Geoffrey Crayon, Gent ······ 141

Unit Ten　Philosophy ··· 143

　Session One　The Daode Jing ··· 144
　Session Two　Metaphysics ··· 150
　Session Three (Extensive Reading)　Is Happiness Still Possible? ······················ 157

参考文献 ··· 162

Unit One Mythology

Lover of myth is in a sense a lover of wisdom.
—Aristotle (Ancient Greek philosopher)

Man today, stripped of myth, stands famished among all his pasts and must dig frantically for roots, be it among the most remote antiquities.
—Friedrich wilhelm Nietzsche (German philosopher)

Myth is not fiction: it consists of facts that are continually repeated and can be observed over and over again. It is something that happens to man, and men have mythical fates just as much as the Greek heroes do.
—Carl Gustav Jung (Swiss psychologist and psychiatrist)

Session One
The Classic of Mountains and Seas (Shan Hai Jing)

ABOUT *THE CLASSIC OF MOUNTAINS AND SEAS*

The Classic of Mountains and Seas is a pre-Qin Chinese classic and also an encyclopedia of prehistoric China. Traditionally ascribed to the mythical figure Yu the Great①, *The Classic of Mountains and Seas* brings together a treasure trove of rare data and colorful fiction about the mythical figures, rituals, natural history, and ethnic peoples of the ancient world.

The book is divided into 18 volumes. It mainly records mountains and seas in the south, west, north, east, and central regions of ancient China. Its rich content covers a range from geographic, religion, zoology, phytology, to mineralogy. This eclectic work contains crucial information on early medicine, omens to avert catastrophe, rites of sacrifice, and familiar and unidentified plants and animals. The whole book documents over 100 countries, 3,000 places, 447 mountains, 300 river courses, 204 mythical figures, 300 strange animals and more than 400 plants.

A lot of ancient myths are also included in the collection, such as the Queen Mother of the West②, Nüwa③, and Kuafu④. These are stories of creation and the beginning of mankind. These stories are now being spread from one generation to another in China. The exact author of the text is not certain nor the exact date it was written. There have been three major viewpoints: one saying is the author being Yu or Bo Yi⑤. The second viewpoint is that the book was probably written by many people in the Warring States Period and was completed in the Western Han Dynasty. Modern scholars said that the book was probably an account of a journey from India to different places in China. The man who wrote the book

---

①Yu the Great: "大禹" in Chinese mythology, the Tamer of the Flood, a savior-hero and reputed founder of China's oldest dynasty, the Xia.

②The Queen Mother of the West: "西王母" in Chinese. Worshipped throughout the continent of Asia, she is one of the oldest and powerful among the Chinese goddesses.

③Nüwa: "女娲" in Chinese. She is a Chinese mythological character best known for creating and reproducing people after a great calamity.

④Kuafu: Kuafu Chasing the Sun (夸父逐日) is one of the earliest famous fables in China. It talks about the legendary story of Kuafu who aspired to catch up with the sun.

⑤A scholar official of the Western Han Dynasty Liu Xin (c. 53 B.C. – 23 A.D.) first put forward this theory. Wang Chong (27 A.D. – 97 A.D.) in the Eastern Han Dynasty believed that Yu was in charge of curbing flood while Bo Yi was in charge of recording strange things and beings.

was called Suichaozi①. Even though the author to the book remains a mystery, the value of this book is definitely unparalleled among ancient Chinese books, due to the variety of its subject and the peculiarity of its content.

READING

卷十二　海内北经(节选)

海内西北陬以东者。②

蛇巫之山，上有人操杯③而东向立。一曰龟山。

西王母梯④几⑤而戴胜杖⑥，其南有三青鸟，为西王母取食。在昆仑虚北。

有人曰大行伯，把戈⑦。其东有犬封国。贰负之尸在大行伯东。

犬封国曰犬戎国，状如犬。有一女子，方跪进杯⑧食。有文马，缟身朱鬣，目若黄金⑨，名曰吉量，乘之寿千岁。

鬼国在贰负之尸北，为物人面而一目。一曰贰负神在其东，为物人面蛇身。⑩

蜪犬如犬，青，食人从首始。

卷十七　大荒北经(节选)

大荒之中，有山名曰不句，海水入焉。

有系昆之山者，有共工之台，射者不敢北乡⑪。有人衣青衣，名曰黄帝女魃⑫。蚩尤⑬作兵

---

①Suichaozi: "随巢子" in Chinese. He was a student of Mozi (墨子) in the Warring State Period.

②The areas which lie east of the northwest comer within the seas.

③"操" means to hold; "杯" equals "棓", a club.

④"梯": lean on/against.

⑤"几": a long and narrow table.

⑥"戴胜": wearing a special piece of jewelry on the head.

⑦"把" means to hold; "戈" means a dagger-axe.

⑧"杯" equals "杯", food and drink. Here the woman is kneeling down to present wine and food.

⑨There is a patterned horse called Wenma which has a white body and a bright red mane, with eyes shining like gold.

⑩The people in the first kingdom all have a human face and only one eye. The people in the second kingdom all have a human face and a snake's body.

⑪Bowmen dare not to shoot arrows in the direction of the north.

⑫"黄帝女魃": also known as "Ba" (魃), which is her proper name, with the nü being an added indication of being feminine. She is the goddess of the drought in Chinese mythology, the daughter of Huangdi. She always wears green clothes.

⑬"蚩尤" was a tribal leader of the ancient Jiuli tribe (九黎). He is best known as the tyrant who fought against the then-future Huangdi in Chinese mythology.

伐黄帝①,黄帝乃令应龙②攻之冀州之野。应龙畜水,蚩尤请风伯雨师,纵大风雨。黄帝乃下天女曰魃,雨止,遂杀蚩尤。魃不得复上,所居不雨③。叔均言之帝,后置之赤水之北。叔均乃为田祖。魃时亡之。所欲逐之者,令曰:"神北行!"④先除⑤水道,决通沟渎⑥。

有人方食鱼,名曰深目民之国,盼姓,食鱼。

有钟山者。有女子衣青衣,名曰赤水女子献。

卷十八 海内经(节选)

淫梁,淫梁生番禺,是始为⑦舟。番禺生奚仲,奚仲生吉光,吉光是始以木为车。

少暤生般,般是始为弓矢。

帝俊赐羿彤弓素矰⑧,以扶下国,羿是始去恤⑨下地之百艰。

帝俊生晏龙,晏龙是为琴瑟。

帝俊有子八人,是始为歌舞。

帝俊生三身,三身生义均,义均是始为巧倕⑩,是始作下民百巧。后稷是播百谷。稷之孙曰叔均,是始作牛耕。大比赤阴,是始为国⑪。禹、鲧是始布土⑫,均定九州。炎帝之妻,赤水之子⑬听訞生炎居,炎居生节并,节并生戏器,戏器生祝融,祝融降处于江水⑭,生共工,共工生术器,术器首方颠⑮,是复土穰,以处江水。共工生后土,后土生噎鸣,噎鸣生岁十有二⑯。

洪水滔天,鲧窃帝之息壤以堙洪水,不待帝命⑰。帝令祝融杀鲧于羽郊。鲧复生禹,帝乃命禹卒⑱布土以定九州。

---

①"黄帝": formally Xuanyuan Huangdi, third of ancient China's mythological emperors, a culture hero and patron saint of Daoism. Huangdi himself is credited with defeating "barbarians"(蚩尤) in a great battle somewhere in what is now Hebei—the victory winning him the leadership of tribes throughout the Huang He plain.

②"应龙": a yellow or golden winged dragon in Chinese mythology who follows Huangdi's order.

③Nüba was unable to go back to heaven and the place she stayed always suffered from a drought.

④Later Shujun was in charge of farming fields. Nüba always desired to run away. Those who tied to drive her away often shouted this command: "The goddess, go north!"

⑤"除": clear and reopen.

⑥"决通沟渎": to connect the ditches.

⑦"始为": to invent.

⑧"彤弓素矰": a red bow and arrows with white feathers.

⑨"恤": to show pity.

⑩Yijun was also called Qiaochui.

⑪Dabichiyin was the first to rule a kingdom.

⑫"布土": to delimit the boundary and settle the territory.

⑬Here refers to "daughter".

⑭Zhurong came down on earth and lived by the Yangtze River.

⑮"首方颠": flat head.

⑯Yeming gave birth to twelve sons who were named after twelve months.

⑰The great flood inundated the whole continent. Gun stole from the God of Heaven of the divine soil to curb the flood.

⑱"卒": at long last.

Session Two *Iliad*

Homer

ABOUT THE AUTHOR

Homer is the presumed author of the *Iliad* and the *Odyssey*①. Although these two great epic poems of ancient Greece have traditionally been attributed to this blind poet, little is known of him beyond the fact that his was the name attached in antiquity by the Greeks themselves to the poems. Some scholars believe him to be one man; others think these iconic stories were created by a group. A variation on the group idea stems from the fact that storytelling was an oral tradition and Homer compiled the stories, then recited them to memory.

Homer's style, whoever he was, falls more in the category of minstrel poet or balladeer, as opposed to a cultivated poet who is the product of a fervent literary moment, such as Virgil② or Shakespeare. The stories have repetitive elements, almost like a chorus or refrain, which suggests a musical element. However, Homer's works are designated as epic rather than lyric poetry, which was originally recited with a lyre③ in hand, much in the same vein as spoken-word performances.

Homer's real life may remain a mystery, but the very real impact of his works continues to illuminate our world today.

ABOUT *ILIAD*

The *Iliad* is composed of 15,693 hexameters④ and is divided into 24 books. The *Iliad* takes place over 51 days during the tenth and final year of the Trojan War. The poem takes its name from the city of Troy, which is also known as Ilium. It is a story of the Achaean⑤ hero Achilles⑥.

---

①The Odyssey recounts the long, adventure-packed sea journey undertaken by Odysseus, a resourceful hero of the Trojan War, in his effort to return to his home and family, and reassume his authority as a king of Ithaca.

②Virgil was regarded by the Romans as their greatest poet, an estimation that subsequent generations have upheld. He is best known for his national epic, the *Aeneid*.

③Lyre: a Greek stringed instrument.

④hexameters: lines of verse, referring to a line of poetry with six main beats.

⑤Achaean: referring to ancient Greek people. Their area as described by Homer—the mainland and western isles of Greece, Crete, Rhodes, and adjacent isles, except the Cyclades—is precisely that covered by the activities of the Mycenaeans in the 14th – 13th century B.C., as revealed by archaeology.

⑥Achilles: in Greek mythology, son of the mortal Peleus, king of the Myrmidons, and the Nereid, or sea nymph, Thetis. He is great warrior of the army of Agamemnon in the Trojan War.

Highlights include: the lengthy Catalog of Ships of the Greek invading forces, the death of Patroclus①(Book 18) and the description of the shield of Achilles②(Book 19), the fight between Achilles and Hector③, and the reconciliation between Achilles and Priam④. In all of these events the intervention of the Greek gods, especially Athena⑤ on the side of the Greeks and Apollo⑥ for the Trojans, is instrumental in the outcome of all of the human actions during the war.

Achilles is part-god and part-man. This Greek superhero is also a psychologically complex character, so the emotion he exhibits—anger, love, rage and grief—are wholly human. The plot of the *Iliad* turns on Achilles' decision to take action that will bring glory to his warrior and to himself. The importance of heroic action in proving virtue, or excellence, is central to the *Iliad* and to the male-dominated culture of the Heroic Age.

The language of the *Iliad*, no less than its theme, is charged with heroic vigor. It makes use of vivid similes, graphic epithets and lengthy catalogs. Its majestic poetry and its heroic personalities have inspired generations of Western Writers.

READING

Book 18(1 – 42, 82 – 150)⑦

So the men fought on like a mass of whirling fire⑧
as swift Antilochus raced the message toward Achilles.
Sheltered under his curving, beaked ships he found him,
foreboding, deep down, all that had come to pass.
Agonizing now he probed his own great heart—
"Why, why? Our long-haired Achaeans routed again,
driven in terror off the plain to crowd the ships, but why?

---

① Patroclus: Achilles' favorite companion and friend.

② The shield of Achilles: it is the shield that Achilles used during his duel against Hector towards the end of the Trojan War. The shield was described in detail by Homer in Iliad.

③ Hector: Hector was a prince of Troy, son of Priam. He was considered the greatest warrior of Troy, and he did not approve of the war that had started between the Greeks and the Trojans.

④ Priam: the king of Troy at the time the Greeks launched an attack against the city, known as the Trojan War.

⑤ Athena: considered to be the city protectress, goddess of war, handicraft, and practical reason in Greek religion, also identified by the Romans with Minerva.

⑥ Apollo: Son of Zeus. He was the God of the arts, music, healing, purification, prophecy, oracles, plague, poetry, civilization, the sun, truth, intelligence, logic, reason, and archery, and he also showed men the art of medicine.

⑦ The excerpts of the *Iliad* in this book are based on a 1990 translation by Robert Fagles, a renowned translator of Greek classics.

⑧ This is connected with the earlier part of last Book, the regular narrative being interrupted by the message of Antilochus and the lamentations of Achilles.

Dear gods, don't bring to pass the grief that haunts my heart—
the prophecy that mother revealed to me one time…
she said the best of the Myrmidons①—while I lived—
would fall at Trojan hands and leave the light of day.
And now he's dead, I know it. Menoetius' gallant son②,
my headstrong friend! And I told Patroclus clearly,
'Once you have beaten off the lethal fire, quick,
come back to the ships—you must not battle Hector!'"
As such fears went churning through his mind
the warlord Nestor③'s son drew near him now,
streaming warm tears, to give the dreaded message:
"Ah son of royal Peleus, what you must hear from me!
What painful news—would to god it had never happened!
Patroclus has fallen. They're fighting over his corpse.
He's stripped, naked—Hector with that flashing helmet,
Hector has your arms!"
                    So the captain reported.
A black cloud of grief came shrouding over Achilles.
Both hands clawing the ground for soot and filth,
he poured it over his head, fouled his handsome face
and black ashes settled onto his fresh clean war-shirt.
Overpowered in all his power, sprawled in the dust,
Achilles lay there, fallen…
tearing his hair, defiling it with his own hands.
And the women he and Patroclus carried off as captives
caught the grief in their hearts and keened and wailed,
out of the tents they ran to ring the great Achilles,
all of them beat their breasts with clenched fists,
sank to the ground, each woman's knees gave way.
Antilochus kneeling near, weeping uncontrollably,

---

①Myrmidons: the name by which the subject warriors of Peleus and Achilles are known in Homer. It derives from Greek word for ants, the creature out of which Zeus was said to have created the in habitants of the island of Aegina, ruled by Peleus.

②Here refers to Patroclus, Achilles' closet friend. He is the son of Menoetius (a Titan god) in Greek mythology.

③Nestor: the son of Neleus, king of Pylos (Navarino) in Elis, and of Chloris. Along with his two sons, he participated in the Trojan War, on the side of the Achaeans. Although he was already at a very old age and did not actively fight in the war, he often spoke to reconcile the Greeks, such as when Agamemnon and Achilles had a dispute.

clutched Achilles' hands as he wept his proud heart out—
for fear he would slash his throat with an iron blade.
Achilles suddenly loosed a terrible, wrenching cry
and his noble mother heard him, seated near her father,
the Old Man of the Sea① in the salt green depths,
and she cried out in turn.

As he groaned from the depths his mother rose before him
and sobbing a sharp cry, cradled her son's head in her hands
and her words were all compassion, winging pity: "My child—
why in tears? What sorrow has touched your heart?
Tell me, please. Don't harbor it deep inside you.
Zeus② has accomplished everything you wanted,
just as you raised your hands and prayed that day.
All the sons of Achaea are pinned against the ships
and all for want of you-they suffer shattering losses."

  And groaning deeply the matchless runner answered,
"O dear mother, true! All those burning desires
Olympian Zeus has brought to pass for me—
but what joy to me now? My dear comrade's dead—
Patroclus—the man I loved beyond all other comrades,
loved as my own life—I've lost him—Hector's killed him,
stripped the gigantic armor off his back, a marvel to behold—
my burnished gear! Radiant gifts the gods presented Peleus
that day they drove you into a mortal's marriage bed…
I wish you'd lingered deep with the deathless sea-nymphs,
lived at ease, and Peleus carried home a mortal bride.
But now, as it is, sorrows, unending sorrows must surge
within your heart as well—for your own son's death.
Never again will you embrace him striding home.
My spirit rebels—I've lost the will to live,
to take my stand in the world of men—unless,
before all else, Hector's battered down by my spear

---

  ①The Old Man of the Sea: a sea god, the father of some fifty to a hundred daughters, including Thetis, mother of Achilles.
  ②Zeus: the father (i.e., the ruler and protector) of both gods and men. He is a sky and weather god, who is also known as Jupiter in Roman mythology.

and gasps away his life, the blood-price for Patroclus,
Menoetius' gallant son he's killed and stripped!"

But Thetis answered, warning through her tears,
"You're doomed to a short life, my son, from all you say!①
For hard on the heels of Hector's death your death
must come at once—"
                    "Then let me die at once"—
Achilles burst out, despairing—"since it was not my fate
to save my dearest comrade from his death! Look,
a world away from his fatherland he's perished,
lacking me, my fighting strength, to defend him.
But now, since I shall not return to my fatherland…
nor did I bring one ray of hope to my Patroclus,
nor to the rest of all my steadfast comrades,
countless ranks struck down by mighty Hector—
No, no, here I sit by the ships…
a useless, dead weight on the good green earth—
I, no man my equal among the bronze-armed Achaeans,
not in battle, only in wars of words that others win.
If only strife could die from the lives of gods and men
and anger that drives the sanest man to flare in outrage—
bitter gall, sweeter than dripping streams of honey,
that swarms in people's chests and blinds like smoke—
just like the anger Agamemnon② king of men
has roused within me now…
                    Enough.
Let bygones be bygones. Done is done.
Despite my anguish I will beat it down,
the fury mounting inside me, down by force.
But now I'll go and meet that murderer head-on,
that Hector who destroyed the dearest life I know.

---

①An oracle had told Thetis that his son Achilles would die young in battle. Thetis was extraordinarily concerned about her baby son's mortality, so she dipped Achilles in the waters of the River Styx, by which means he became invulnerable, except for the part of his heel by which she held him. This is where the proverb "Achilles' heel" comes from.

②Agamemnon: King of Mycenae (prehistoric Greek city in the Peloponnese). He led the Greek forces in the Trojan War.

For my own death, I'll meet it freely—whenever Zeus
and the other deathless gods would like to bring it on!
Not even Heracles fled his death, for all his power,
favorite son as he was to Father Zeus the King.
Fate crushed him, and Hera's savage anger.
And I too, if the same fate waits for me...
I'll lie in peace, once I've gone down to death.
But now, for the moment, let me seize great glory!—
and drive some woman of Troy or deep-breasted Dardan
to claw with both hands at her tender cheeks and wipe away
her burning tears as the sobs come choking from her throat—
they'll learn that I refrained from war a good long time!
Don't try to hold me back from the fighting, mother,
love me as you do. You can't persuade me now."

Book 19 (423 – 477)[①]

Thick-and-fast as the snow comes swirling down from Zeus,
frozen sharp when the North Wind born in heaven blasts it on—
so massed, so dense the glistening burnished helmets shone,
streaming out of the ships, and shields with jutting bosses,
breastplates welded front and back and the long ashen spears.
The glory of armor lit the skies and the whole earth laughed,
rippling under the glitter of bronze, thunder resounding
under trampling feet of armies. And in their midst
the brilliant Achilles began to arm for battle...
A sound of grinding came from the fighter's teeth,
his eyes blazed forth in searing points of fire,
unbearable grief came surging through his heart
and now, bursting with rage against the men of Troy,
he donned Hephaestus[②]' gifts—magnificent armor
the god of fire forged with all his labor.
First he wrapped his legs with well-made greaves,
fastened behind his heels with silver ankle-clasps,
next he strapped the breastplate round his chest
then over his shoulder Achilles slung his sword,
the fine bronze blade with its silver-studded hilt,
then hoisted the massive shield flashing far and wide

[①] In the following excerpts of Book 19, Achilles prepares to lead the Achaeans into battle.
[②] Hephaestus: the god of fire and of metalworking, who has forged a special set of arms for Achilles.

Unit One Mythology

like a full round moon—and gleaming bright as the light
that reaches sailors out at sea, the flare of a watchfire
burning strong in a lonely sheepfold up some mountain slope
when the gale-winds hurl the crew that fights against them
far over the fish-swarming sea, far from loved ones—
so the gleam from Achilles' well-wrought blazoned shield
shot up and hit the skies. Then lifting his rugged helmet
he set it down on his brows, and the horsehair crest
shone like a star and the waving golden plumes shook
that Hephaestus drove in bristling thick along its ridge.
And brilliant Achilles tested himself in all his gear,
Achilles spun on his heels to see if it fitted tightly,
see if his shining limbs ran free within it, yes,
and it felt like buoyant wings lifting the great captain.
And then, last, Achilles drew his father's spear
from its socket-stand—weighted, heavy, tough.
No other Achaean fighter could heft that shaft,
only Achilles had the skill to wield it well:
Pelian ash it was, a gift to his father Peleus
presented by Chiron① once, hewn on Pelion's crest
to be the death of heroes.
                                        Now the war-team—
Alcimus and Automedon② worked to yoke them quickly.
They cinched the supple breast-straps round their chests
and driving the bridle irons home between their jaws,
pulled the reins back taut to the bolted chariot.
Seizing a glinting whip, his fist on the handgrip,
Automedon leapt aboard behind the team and behind him
Achilles struck his stance, helmed for battle now,
glittering in his armor like the sun astride the skies,
his ringing, daunting voice commanding his father's horses:
"Roan Beauty and Charger, illustrious foals of Lightfoot!
Try hard, do better this time—bring your charioteer

---

　①Chiron: A centaur (half-man, half horse), one of the creatures driven from Mount Pelion by the Lapiths (a mountain tribe in the northern Greece).
　②Alcimus and Automedon: companions of Achilles. Both were Myrmidon Captains and were the two most favored by Achilles after Patroclus' death.

back home alive to his waiting Argive① comrades
once we're through with fighting. Don't leave Achilles
there on the battlefield as you left Patroclus—dead!"

COMPREHENSION & EXERCISES

Ⅰ. *The Classic of Mountains and Seas* **records many magic animals and deities of mountain ranges with different bodies. Find the corresponding descriptions of the following terms and explain them in English.**

青鸟

文马

鬼国

贰负神

蜪犬

Ⅱ. **Translate the following lines from the** *Iliad* **(Book 19) which illustrates the armor of Achilles, including his famous shield.**

First he wrapped his legs with well-made greaves,
fastened behind his heels with silver ankle-clasps,
next he strapped the breastplate round his chest
then over his shoulder Achilles slung his sword,
the fine bronze blade with its silver-studded hilt,
then hoisted the massive shield flashing far and wide
like a full round moon—and gleaming bright as the light
that reaches sailors out at sea, the flare of a watchfire
burning strong in a lonely sheepfold up some mountain slope
when the gale-winds hurl the crew that fights against them
far over the fish-swarming sea, far from loved ones—
so the gleam from Achilles' well-wrought blazoned shield
shot up and hit the skies. Then lifting his rugged helmet
he set it down on his brows, and the horsehair crest
shone like a star and the waving golden plumes shook
that Hephaestus drove in bristling thick along its ridge.
And brilliant Achilles tested himself in all his gear,
Achilles spun on his heels to see if it fitted tightly,
see if his shining limbs ran free within it, yes,
and it felt like buoyant wings lifting the great captain.
And then, last, Achilles drew his father's spear
from its socket-stand—weighted, heavy, tough.

---

①Argive: an alternate name for an Archaen or Greek in general.

III. **Discuss the following questions.**

1. *The Classic of Mountains and Seas* records many ancient Chinese myths and legends, including myths of creation of the universe, of invention and creation, and of wars. Identify each myth in the excerpts and explain how they reflect the heroic spirit of Chinese people. Can you also think of some other famous legends from ancient China?

2. Both Chinese and Greek goddesses have played a crucial part in ancient mythology. Compare and contrast the personalities and roles they serve in the story and explain how they have been portrayed differently.

3. After Antilochus races to Achilles' camp to bring him the news of Patroclus' death, Achilles is devastated. Later, he decides to lead the Achaeans into the battle. How would you describe the personality of Achilles based on the description in Book 18?

4. Homer is known for using vivid similes and graphic description, find some examples in the above excerpts and explain how these techniques can help with the storytelling?

5. In both Chinese and Greek mythology, the intervention of deities is instrumental in the outcome of all of the human actions during the war. Compare both works and explain how heroes collaborate with deities.

6. Read Volume 17 of *The Classic of Mountains and Seas* and the *Iliad*, and compare the narratives in both works when it comes to illustrate the tale of war.

IV. **Writing task.**

Read Volume 17 *The Classic of the Great Wilderness: the North* again, and write your own version of this ancient Chinese story.

Session Three (Extensive Reading) *Theogony*[①]

Hesiod

[116] Verily at the first Chaos came to be, but next wide-bosomed Earth, the ever-sure foundations of all the deathless ones who hold the peaks of snowy Olympus, and dim Tartarus in the depth of the wide-pathed Earth, and Eros (Love), fairest among the deathless gods, who unnerves the limbs and overcomes the mind and wise counsels of all gods and all men within them. From Chaos came forth Erebus and black Night; but of Night were born Aether and Day, whom she conceived and bare from union in love with Erebus. And Earth first bare starry Heaven, equal to herself, to cover her on every side, and to be an ever-sure abiding-place for the blessed gods. And she brought forth long Hills, graceful haunts of the goddess-Nymphs who dwell amongst the glens of the hills. She bare also the fruitless deep with his raging swell, Pontus, without sweet union of love.

[134] But afterwards she lay with Heaven and bare deep-swirling Oceanus, Coeus and Crius and Hyperion and Iapetus, Theia and Rhea, Themis and Mnemosyne and gold-crowned Phoebe and lovely Tethys. After them was born Cronos the wily, youngest and most terrible of her children, and he hated his lusty sire.

[139] And again, she bare the Cyclopes, overbearing in spirit, Brontes, and Steropes and stubborn-hearted Arges, who gave Zeus the thunder and made the thunderbolt: in all else they were like the gods, but one eye only was set in the midst of their fore-heads. And they were surnamed Cyclopes (Orb-eyed) because one orbed eye was set in their foreheads. Strength and might and craft were in their works.

[147] And again, three other sons were born of Earth and Heaven, great and doughty beyond telling, Cottus and Briareos and Gyes, presumptuous children. From their shoulders sprang an hundred arms, not to be approached, and each had fifty heads upon his shoulders on their strong limbs, and irresistible was the stubborn strength that was in their great forms. For of all the children that were born of Earth and Heaven, these were the most terrible, and they were hated by their own father from the first. And he used to hide them

---

[①] Excerpts from Hesiod's *Theogony*, translated by Hugh, G Everlyn-White (a translator of Greek epic poetry) and published in 1914. Hesiod is one of the earliest Greek poets, often called the "father of Greek didactic poetry". Two of his complete epics have survived, *Theogony* and *Works and Days*. The *Theogony* recounts the history and genealogy of the gods, and along with the works of Homer, is one of the key source documents for Greek mythology. It gives the clearest presentation of the Greek pagan creation myths, starting with the creatrix goddesses Chaos and Earth. It also mentions hundreds of individual gods, goddesses, demi-gods and heroes.

all away in a secret place of Earth so soon as each was born, and would not suffer them to come up into the light: and Heaven rejoiced in his evil doing. But vast Earth groaned within, being straitened, and she made the element of grey flint and shaped a great sickle, and told her plan to her dear sons.

[163] And she spoke, cheering them, while she was vexed in her dear heart: "My children, gotten of a sinful father, if you will obey me, we should punish the vile outrage of your father; for he first thought of doing shameful things."

[167] So she said; but fear seized them all, and none of them uttered a word. But great Cronos the wily took courage and answered his dear mother: "Mother, I will undertake to do this deed, for I reverence not our father of evil name, for he first thought of doing shameful things."

[173] So he said: and vast Earth rejoiced greatly in spirit, and set and hid him in an ambush, and put in his hands a jagged sickle, and revealed to him the whole plot.

[176] And Heaven came, bringing on night and longing for love, and he lay about Earth spreading himself full upon her.

[177] Then the son from his ambush stretched forth his left hand and in his right took the great long sickle with jagged teeth, and swiftly lopped off his own father's members and cast them away to fall behind him. And not vainly did they fall from his hand; for all the bloody drops that gushed forth Earth received, and as the seasons moved round she bare the strong Erinyes and the great Giants with gleaming armour, holding long spears in their hands and the Nymphs whom they call Meliae8 all over the boundless earth. And so soon as he had cut off the members with flint and cast them from the land into the surging sea, they were swept away over the main a long time: and a white foam spread around them from the immortal flesh, and in it there grew a maiden. First she drew near holy Cythera, and from there, afterwards, she came to sea-girt Cyprus, and came forth an awful and lovely goddess, and grass grew up about her beneath her shapely feet. Her gods and men call Aphrodite, and the foam-born goddess and rich-crowned Cytherea, because she grew amid the foam, and Cytherea because she reached Cythera, and Cyprogenes because she was born in billowy Cyprus, and Philommedes9 because sprang from the members. And with her went Eros, and comely Desire followed her at her birth at the first and as she went into the assembly of the gods. This honour she has from the beginning, and this is the portion allotted to her amongst men and undying gods, —the whisperings of maidens and smiles and deceits with sweet delight and love and graciousness.

[207] But these sons whom be begot himself great Heaven used to call Titans (Strainers) in reproach, for he said that they strained and did presumptuously a fearful deed, and that vengeance for it would come afterwards.

[211] And Night bare hateful Doom and black Fate and Death, and she bare Sleep and the tribe of Dreams. And again the goddess murky Night, though she lay with none, bare Blame and painful Woe, and the Hesperides who guard the rich, golden apples and the trees

bearing fruit beyond glorious Ocean. Also she bare the Destinies and ruthless avenging Fates, Clotho and Lachesis and Atropos, who give men at their birth both evil and good to have, and they pursue the transgressions of men and of gods: and these goddesses never cease from their dread anger until they punish the sinner with a sore penalty. Also deadly Night bare Nemesis (Indignation) to afflict mortal men, and after her, Deceit and Friendship and hateful Age and hard-hearted Strife.

[226] But abhorred Strife bare painful Toil and Forgetfulness and Famine and tearful Sorrows, Fightings also, Battles, Murders, Manslaughters, Quarrels, Lying Words, Disputes, Lawlessness and Ruin, all of one nature, and Oath who most troubles men upon earth when anyone wilfully swears a false oath.

[233] And Sea begat Nereus, the eldest of his children, who is true and lies not: and men call him the Old Man because he is trusty and gentle and does not forget the laws of righteousness, but thinks just and kindly thoughts. And yet again he got great Taumas and proud Phoreys, being mated with Earth, and fair-cheeked Ceto and Eurybia who has a heart of flint within her.

Unit Two　　Society

身修而后家齐,家齐而后国治,国治而后天下平。

————孔子(中国哲学家、思想家)

Their persons being cultivated, their families were regulated. Their families being regulated, their states were rightly governed. Their states being rightly governed, the whole kingdom was made tranquil and happy.

—Confucius (Chinese philosopher & thinker)

For the mere impulse of appetite is slavery, while obedience to a law which we prescribe to ourselves is liberty.

—Jean-Jacques Rousseau (French philosopher)

Ethnic groups are those human groups that entertain a subjective belief in their common descent because of similarities of physical type or of customs or both, or because of memories of colonization or migration; this belief must be important for the propagation of group formation; conversely, it does not matter whether or not an objective blood relationship exists.

—Max Weber (German sociologist & philosopher)

Session One
The Peach Blossom Spring (Taohuayuan Ji)

Tao Yuanming

ABOUT THE AUTHOR

　　Tao Yuanming (365A. D. - 427A. D.) was the greatest Chinese hermit poet, and his pastoral poems occupy a glorious place in the history of Chinese poetry. Tao Yuanming, with the courtesy name of Yuanliang, the given name of Qian, the alternative courtesy name of Yuanming and the alias of Mr. Wuliu, was born in a declining bureaucratic family. Tao Yuanming took a minor official post while in his 20s in order to support his aged parents. After about 10 years at that post and a brief term as county magistrate, he resigned from official life, repelled by its excessive formality and widespread corruption. With his wife and children he retired to a farming village south of the Yangtze River. Despite the hardships of a farmer's life and frequent food shortages, Tao was contented, writing poetry, cultivating the chrysanthemums that became inseparably associated with his poetry, and drinking wine, also a common subject of his verse.

　　Tao Yuanming's seclusion was of important and peculiar significance in the history of Chinese literature. First, Tao Yuanming's resignation from his official post and seclusion truly revealed his real personality, showed his thorough understanding of the dark side of the society, the dirty officialdom and life values, and manifested the poet's unique state of life and peculiar understanding of art. All people in the world deem "Ah, homeward bound I go" as Tao Yuanming's expression of his true feelings about seclusion:

　　Ah, homeward bound I go! Why not go home, seeing that my field and gardens are overgrown? Myself have made my soul serf to my body: why have vain regrets and mourn alone? Fret not over bygones and the forward journey take. Only a short distance have I gone astray, and I know today I am right, if yesterday was a complete mistake. Lightly floats and drifts the boat, and the wind gently flows and flaps my gown. I inquire the road of a wayfarer, and sulk at the dimness of the dawn.

　　Here, Tao Yuanming clearly revealed his determination to leave officialdom and never make "my soul serf to my body." He wanted to live free and indulged in imagining how free and happy he would become after leaving officialdom and returning to the countryside! "Ah, homeward bound I go" is not a real description of the life of Tao Yuanming as a recluse but a description of how he felt when he had just decided to become a hermit and his aspiration to future life. Though this article is short, it has the style and beauty of metrical composition and is plain like all other poems by Tao Yuanming.

Tao Yuanming's seclusion itself also had special connotations. Tao's seclusion was not a strategy. He really became a hermit and realized his life values in seclusion. Therefore, after becoming a hermit, he never wanted to become an official again and devoted himself to rural life wholeheartedly. People said that Tao Yuanming kindly communicated with farmers as their equal. Actually he had completely turned himself into a farmer. He did farm work and tilled land himself, not only suffering hardships, but also tasting the sweet. He laid a foundation for rural life through his labor and enjoyed unparalleled joy of life in this course. This is shown in the first of Five Poems of "Back to Pastoral Life":

> I've loathed the madding crowd since I was a boy
> While hills and mountains have filled me with joy.
> By mistake I sought mundane careers
> And got entrapped in them for thirty years.
> Birds in the cage would long for wooded hills;
> Fish in the pond would yearn for flowing rills.
> So I reclaim the land in southern fields
> To suit my bent for reaping farmland yields.
> My farm contains a dozen mu of ground;
> My cottage has eight or nine rooms around.
> The elm and willow cover backside eaves
> While peach and plum trees shade my yard with leaves.
> The distant village dimly looms somewhere,
> With smoke from chimneys drifting in the air
> In silent country lanes a stray dog barks;
> Amid the mulberry trees cocks crow with larks.
>
> My house is free from worldly moil or gloom
> While ease and quiet permeate my private room.
> When I escape from bitter strife with men,
> I live a free and easy life again.

This poem truly portrays the happy mood and tranquil life after the poet's return to the countryside. After reflecting on his "entry into the secular world by mistake" 30 years before, the poet described his contentment and amusement in the countryside, the farm, cottage, the elm and willow, peach and plum trees, a barking dog and crowing cocks in natural and harmonious scene in detail. Of course, more importantly, people can feel how pure and happy the poet's state of mind was.

ABOUT "THE PEACH BLOSSOM SPRING"

"The Peach Blossom Spring" was a fable written by Tao Yuanming in 421A.D. about a chance discovery of an ethereal utopia where the people led an ideal existence in harmony with nature, unaware of the outside world for centuries.

Tao lived during a time of political instability and national disunity. The story describes how a fisherman haphazardly sailed into a stream in a forest made up entirely of blossoming peach trees, where even the ground was covered by peach petals. When he reached the end of the stream, he found a grotto. Though narrow at first, he was able to squeeze through and the passage eventually reached a hidden village.

The villagers were surprised to see him, but were kind and friendly. They explained that their ancestors escaped to this place during the civil unrest of the Qin dynasty (221B.C.–207B.C.) and they themselves had not left since or had contact with anyone from the outside. As a result, they had heard nothing of subsequent changes in political regimes.

The fisherman was warmly received by the hospitable villagers and stayed for over a week. Upon leaving, he was informed that it was worthless to reveal this experience to the outside world. However, he marked his route on his way out with signs and later divulged the existence of this idyllic haven to others. They tried to find it repeatedly but in vain.

Since then, the peach blossom spring has become a popular symbol of an ideal world in the hearts of the Chinese people. The story inspired many later poems, paintings and music compositions.

READING

桃花源记

陶渊明

晋太元中,武陵人捕鱼为业,缘溪行,忘路之远近。忽逢桃花林,夹岸数百步①,中无杂树,芳草鲜美,落英缤纷②。渔人甚异之。复前行,欲穷其林。

林尽水源,便得一山。山有小口,仿佛若有光。便舍船从口入。初极狭,才通人。复行数

---

①Peaches are famous in China for being the fruit of the immortals. So with the fisherman's early discovery of peach orchards, we know that we have entered a magical and spiritual place. Springheads and water sources are places where the water, and life itself, are pure and transparent.

②This sentence describes how the fisherman came across the peach blossom spring: he suddenly chanced upon a peach blossom forest; keeping by the shore he moved a hundred paces; inside there were no other trees, and the fragrant grasses were fresh and beautiful; the fallen leaves were a mix of colors.

十步,豁然开朗。土地平旷,屋舍俨然①。有良田、美池、桑竹之属②。阡陌交通③,鸡犬相闻。其中往来种作,男女衣着,悉如外人。黄发垂髫④,并怡然自乐。见渔人,乃大惊,问所从来,具⑤答之。便要还家,设酒杀鸡作食⑥。村中闻有此人,咸来问讯。自云先世避秦时乱,率妻子邑人来此绝境,不复出焉,遂与外人间隔⑦。问今是何世,乃不知有汉,无论魏、晋。此人一一为具言所闻,皆叹惋。余人各复延至其家,皆出酒食。停数日,辞去。此中人语云:"不足为外人道也。"

既出,得其船,便扶向路,处处志之。及郡下⑧,诣太守⑨,说如此。太守即遣人随其往,寻向所志,遂迷,不复得路。

南阳刘子骥,高尚士也,闻之,欣然规往,未果,寻病终。后遂无问津者⑩。

Session Two　*The Social Contract*

Jean‑Jacques Rousseau

ABOUT THE AUTHOR

Jean‑Jacques Rousseau remains an important figure in the history of philosophy, both because of his contributions to political philosophy and moral psychology and because of his influence on later thinkers. Rousseau's own view of philosophy and philosophers was firmly negative, seeing philosophers as the post-hoc rationalizers⑪ of self-interest, as apologists for various forms of tyranny, and as playing a role in the alienation of the modern individual from humanity's natural impulse to compassion. The concern that dominates Rousseau's work is to find a way of preserving human freedom in a world where human beings are increasingly dependent on one another for the satisfaction of their needs. This concern has two dimensions: material and psychological, of which the latter has greater importance. In the modern world, human beings

---

① The land was flat and vast with houses and buildings neatly arranged.
② fertile fields, beautiful ponds, trees of mulberry and bamboo.
③ The footpaths between the fields met at intersections.
④ elders and children.
⑤ "具": completely.
⑥ brought out wine, killed chickens and made a meal.
⑦ Former generations fled the chaos in the time of Qin, bringing their wives, children and villagers to this impasse, and they have never left, and so been separated from outsiders.
⑧ "郡下": provincial capital, county seat.
⑨ "太守": governor, senior official.
⑩ There were none who inquired about it.
⑪ Rationalize (redirected from rationalizers): to explain rationally, e. g. "Philosophy is essentially the endeavor of the human mind to rationalize the universe" (Francis Ellingwood Abbot).

come to derive their very sense of self from the opinion of others, a fact which Rousseau sees as corrosive of freedom and destructive of individual authenticity.

His *Discourse on Inequality* and *The Social Contract* are cornerstones in modern political and social thought. Rousseau's sentimental novel *Julie*, or *The New Heloise* was important to the development of pre-romanticism① and romanticism in fiction. Rousseau's autobiographical writings—the posthumously published *Confessions* (composed in 1769), which initiated the modern autobiography, and the unfinished *Reveries of the Solitary Walker* (composed 1776 - 1778)—exemplified the late-18th-century "Age of Sensibility", and featured an increased focus on subjectivity② and introspection that later characterized modern writing.

In his mature work, he principally explores two routes to achieving and protecting freedom: the first is a political one aimed at constructing political institutions that allow for the co-existence of free and equal citizens in a community where they themselves are sovereign; the second is a project for child development and education that fosters autonomy and avoids the development of the most destructive forms of self-interest. However, though Rousseau believes the co-existence of human beings in relations of equality and freedom is possible, he is consistently and overwhelmingly pessimistic that humanity will escape from a dystopia of alienation, oppression, and unfreedom. In addition to his contributions to philosophy, Rousseau was active as a composer and a music theorist, as the pioneer of modern autobiography, as a novelist, and as a botanist. Rousseau's appreciation of the wonders of nature and his stress on the importance of feeling and emotion made him an important influence on and anticipator of the romantic movement. To a very large extent, the interests and concerns that mark his philosophical work also inform these other activities, and Rousseau's contributions in ostensibly non-philosophical fields often serve to illuminate his philosophical commitments and arguments.

ABOUT *THE SOCIAL CONTRACT*

The Social Contract is a treatise published in 1762 by Jean - Jacques Rousseau. It is a cornerstone in modern political and social thought and makes a strong case for democratic government and social empowerment. Rousseau argues about the best ways to establish and maintain political authority without unduly sacrificing personal liberty. *The Social Contract* was enormously influential on political thought before and during the French Revolution.

In the first of four books, Rousseau poses the fundamental problem he hopes to address

---

①Romanticism: an artistic and intellectual movement originating in Europe in the late 1700s and characterized by a heightened interest in nature, emphasis on the individual's expression of emotion and imagination, departure from the attitudes and forms of classicism, and rebellion against established social rules and conventions.

②Subjectivity: judgment based on individual personal impressions and feelings and opinions rather than external facts, e.g. "The sensation of pain is a highly subjective experience that varies by culture as well as by individual temperament and situation" (John Hoberman).

with his treatise: how to build a durable and effective political state without excessively restricting the natural liberties of humankind. Under Rousseau's social contract, the people surrender some of their rights to the "general will", which is the only truly legitimate form of authority. Because each individual gives up the same rights and takes on the same responsibilities, the people remain as free as they could possibly be while living in an ordered society. Essentially, the people trade "natural liberty"—meaning the freedom to take whatever one can at all times—for "civil liberty", which is much more valuable for contemporary, collaborative humankind. According to Rousseau, the social contract also replaces "natural inequality"—meaning, natural disparities in physical and mental capabilities—with "civil equality", in which all individuals are treated the same under the law.

In Book 2, Rousseau explains his concept of the general will. In his view, the general will is indestructible, indivisible, and infallible. Although the people may disagree on what they think it is, the general will remains unchanged. The general will is expressed through laws that apply generally and do not mention specific individuals or groups. The person or persons who write these laws should ideally be outsiders, and the laws should consider the geography of the territory and the temperament of the people.

In Book 3, Rousseau makes an important distinction between sovereign authority, or the general will, and the government, which executes and administers the laws of sovereignty. Rousseau lists three types of government: monarchy, aristocracy and democracy.

Finally, in Book 4, Rousseau touches on miscellaneous topics like voting, the judiciary, temporary dictators and religion. Rousseau recommends that each state adopt a civil religion, Christian or otherwise, made up of simple positive dogmas, like a belief in God, the afterlife, and divine justice.

READING

BOOK I

Chapter I Subject of the First Book

Man is born free; and everywhere he is in chains. One thinks himself the master of others, and still remains a greater slave than they. How did this change come about? I do not know. What can make it legitimate? That question I think I can answer.

If I took into account only force, and the effects derived from it, I should say: "As long as a people is compelled to obey, and obeys, it does well; as soon as it can shake off the yoke[①] and shakes it off, it does still better; for, regaining its liberty by the same right as took it

---

①yoke: rough treatment or something that restricts your freedom and makes your life very difficult to bear.

away, either it is justified in resuming it, or there was no justification for those who took it away."① But the social order is a sacred right which is the basis of all other rights. Nevertheless, this right does not come from nature, and must therefore be founded on conventions.

Chapter Ⅱ　The First Societies

The most ancient of all societies, and the only one that is natural is the family: and even so the children remain attached to the father only so long as they need him for their preservation. As soon as this need ceases, the natural bond is dissolved. The children, released from the obedience they owed to the father, and the father, released from the care he owed his children, return equally to independence. If they remain united, they continue so no longer naturally, but voluntarily; and the family itself is then maintained only by convention.

This common liberty results from the nature of man. His first law is to provide for his own preservation, his first cares are those which he owes to himself; and, as soon as he reaches years of discretion②, he is the sole judge of the proper means of preserving himself, and consequently becomes his own master.

The family then may be called the first model of political societies: the ruler corresponds to the father, and the people to the children; and all, being born free and equal, alienate their liberty only for their own advantage. The whole difference is that, in the family, the love of the father for his children repays him for the care he takes of them, while, in the State, the pleasure of commanding takes the place of the love which the chief③ cannot have for the peoples under him.

Chapter Ⅵ　The Social Compact

I suppose men to have reached the point at which the obstacles in the way of their preservation in the state of nature show their power of resistance to be greater than the resources at the disposal of each individual for his maintenance in that state.④ That primitive condition can then subsist no longer; and the human race would perish unless it changed its manner of existence.

But, as men cannot engender new forces, but only unite and direct existing ones, they have no other means of preserving themselves than the formation, by aggregation, of a sum of forces great enough to overcome the resistance. These they have to bring into play by means of a single motive power, and cause to act in concert⑤.

---

　　①Here the author explains the relationship between power (violence in particular) and freedom.
　　②discretion: the freedom or power to decide what should be done.
　　③chief: a person with a high rank.
　　④This sentence means that in a certain period of human development, the survival of individuals in the state of nature can no longer be maintained by the weak and contemptuous power of single individual, otherwise the state of nature cannot exist anymore. And the solution of this to be united with collective wisdom and efforts.
　　⑤in concert: working together.

This sum of forces can arise only where several persons come together: but, as the force and liberty of each man are the chief instruments of his self-preservation, how can he pledge① them without harming his own interests, and neglecting the care he owes to himself This difficulty, in its bearing on my present subject, may be stated in the following terms— "The problem is to find a form of association which will defend and protect with the whole common force the person and goods of each associate, and in which each, while uniting himself with all, may still obey himself alone, and remain as free as before." This is the fundamental problem of which the Social Contract provides the solution.

   The clauses of this contract are so determined by the nature of the act that the slightest modification would make them vain and ineffective; so that, although they have perhaps never been formally set forth, they are everywhere the same and everywhere tacitly admitted and recognised, until, on the violation of the social compact, each regains his original rights and resumes his natural liberty, while losing the conventional liberty in favour of which he renounced it.②

   These clauses, properly understood, may be reduced to one—the total alienation③ of each associate④, together with all his rights, to the whole community for,⑤ in the first place, as each gives himself absolutely, the conditions are the same for all; and, this being so, no one has any interest in making them burdensome to others.

   Moreover, the alienation being without reserve, the union is as perfect as it can be, and no associate has anything more to demand: for, if the individuals retained certain rights, as there would be no common superior to decide between them and the public, each, being on one point his own judge, would ask to be so on all; the state of nature would thus continue, and the association would necessarily become inoperative or tyrannical.

   Finally, each man, in giving himself to all, gives himself to nobody; and as there is no associate over whom he does not acquire the same right as he yields others over himself, he gains an equivalent for everything he loses, and an increase of force for the preservation of what he has.

   If then we discard from the social compact what is not of its essence, we shall find that it reduces itself to the following terms—"Each of us puts his person and all his power in common under the supreme direction of the general will⑥, and, in our corporate capacity,

---

　①pledge: to make sb or yourself formally promise to do something.

　②This sentence means that the clauses of the social contract should be widely admitted unconditionally, otherwise, if one gives the social compact up, he/she will regain the natural liberty and return to the primitive condition.

　③Here "alienation" refers to (law) the voluntary and absolute transfer of natural liberty/right from individual to the whole society.

　④associate: each member of the society that they work and live with.

　⑤Every member should dedicate their rights to the whole society.

　⑥Rousseau believes that only general will can direct the society towards common good. The idea of the general will is at the heart of Rousseau's philosophy. When individuals have been transformed into a state by enter into social contract, they are united by common goods. The general will is the will of a state as a whole.

we receive each member as an indivisible part of the whole."

At once, in place of the individual personality of each contracting party, this act of association creates a moral and collective body, composed of as many members as the assembly contains votes, and receiving from this act its unity, its common identity, its life and its will. This public person, so formed by the union of all other persons, formerly took the name of city①, and now takes that of Republic or body politic; it is called by its members State when passive, Sovereign when active, and Power when compared with others like itself. Those who are associated in it take collectively the name of people, and severally are called citizens, as sharing in the sovereign power, and subjects, as being under the laws of the State.

Chapter Ⅷ The Civil State

The passage from the state of nature to the civil state produces a very remarkable change in man, by substituting justice, for instinct in his conduct, and giving his actions the morality they had formerly lacked. Then only, when the voice of duty takes the place of physical impulses and right of appetite②, does man, who so far had considered only himself, find that he is forced to act on different principles, and to consult his reason before listening to his inclinations③. Although, in this state, he deprives himself of some advantages which he got from nature, he gains in return others so great, his faculties are so stimulated and developed, his ideas so extended, his feelings so ennobled, and his whole soul so uplifted, that, did not the abuses of this new condition often degrade him below that which he left, he would be bound to bless continually the happy moment which took him from it for ever④, and, instead of a stupid and unimaginative animal, made him an intelligent being and a man.

Let us draw up the whole account in terms easily commensurable. What man loses by the social contract in his natural liberty and an unlimited right to everything he tries to get

---

①Author's note: the real meaning of this word has been almost wholly lost in modern times; most people mistake a town for a city, and a townsman for a citizen. They do not know that houses make a town, but citizens a city. The same mistake long ago cost the Carthaginians dear. I have never read of the title of citizens being given to the subjects of any prince, not even the ancient Macedonians or the English of today, though they are nearer liberty than any one else. The French alone everywhere familiarly adopt the name of citizens, because, as can be seen from their dictionaries, they have no idea of its meaning; otherwise they would be guilty in usurping it, of the crime of lèse-majesté: among them, the name expresses a virtue, and not a right. When Bodin spoke of our citizens and townsmen, he fell into a bad blunder in taking the one class for the other. M. d'Alembert has avoided the error, and, in his article on Geneva, has clearly distinguished the four orders of men (or even five, counting mere foreigners) who dwell in our town, of which two only compose the Republic. No other French writer, to my knowledge, has understood the real meaning of the word citizen.

②right of appetite: power replaces greed.

③inclination: selfish desire.

④This sentence means that as long as this new environment is not destroyed, which makes his life more difficult, people are bound to accept this civil society.

and succeeds in getting; what he gains is civil liberty and the proprietorship of all he possesses.① If we are to avoid mistake in weighing one against the other, we must clearly distinguish natural liberty, which is bounded only by the strength of the individual, from civil liberty, which is limited by the general will;② and possession, which is merely the effect of force or the right of the first occupier, from property, which can be founded only on a positive title.

We might, over and above all this, add, to what man acquires in the civil state, moral liberty③, which alone makes him truly master of himself; for the mere impulse of appetite is slavery, while obedience to a law which we prescribe to ourselves is liberty. But I have already said too much on this head, and the philosophical meaning of the word liberty does not now concern us.

BOOK II

Chapter Ⅵ Law④

By the social compact we have given the body politic existence and life: we have now by legislation to give it movement and will. For the original act by which the body is formed and united still in no respect determines what it ought to do for its preservation.

When I say that the object of laws is always general, I mean that law considers subjects en masse⑤ and actions in the abstract, and never a particular person or action. Thus the law may indeed decree that there shall be privileges, but cannot confer them on anybody by name. It may set up several classes of citizens, and even lay down the qualifications for membership of these classes, but it cannot nominate such and such persons as belonging to them; it may establish a monarchical government and hereditary succession, but it cannot choose a king, or nominate a royal family. In a word, no function which has a particular object belongs to the legislative power.

On this view, we at once see that it can no longer be asked whose business it is to make

---

①What a man loses is his/her natural liberty and unrestricted right to everything he takes, but what he/she obtains is the freedom of citizens and the ownership of private property.

②Natural liberty, as Rousseau states, is the freedom to pursue one's own desires whereas civil liberty is the freedom to pursue the general will.

③Rousseau identifies moral liberty as a form of positive freedom, whereby one's actions conform to one's own true will. Moral freedom would thus be realized if each individual has himself willed the laws of his polity.

④Rousseau is convinced that laws could not be unjust if the general will of the people was followed. the belief that freedom and civil liberty are essential to a just society. Society should not be ruled by elites but by the general will of all people.

⑤en masse: in a group; all together.

laws, since they are acts of the general will: nor whether the prince is above the law, since he is a member of the State; nor whether the law can be unjust, since no one is unjust to himself; nor how we can be both free and subject to the laws since they are but registers of our wills.

We see further that, as the law unites universality of will with universality of object, what a man, whoever he be, commands of his own motion cannot be a law; and even what the Sovereign commands with regard to a particular matter is no nearer being a law, but is a decree①, an act, not of sovereignty②, but of magistracy③.

Laws are, properly speaking, only the conditions of civil association. The people, being subject to the laws, ought to be their author. Of itself the people wills always the good, but of itself it by no means always sees it. The general will is always in the right, but the judgment which guides it is not always enlightened.④ The individuals see the good they reject; the public wills the good it does not see. All stand equally in need of guidance. The former must be compelled to bring their wills into conformity with their reason; the latter must be taught to know what it wills. If that is done, public enlightenment leads to the union of understanding and will in the social body: the parts are made to work exactly together, and the whole is raised to its highest power. This makes a legislator necessary.

COMPREHENSION & EXERCISES

Ⅰ. Read "The Peach Blossom Spring" and try to explain the following terms in English.

隐居

田园诗

桃花源

桃李

守拙

落英缤纷

Ⅱ. Read *The Social Contract* and choose the best answers for the following questions.

1. According to Rousseau, what is legitimate political authority based on?

    A. Slavery   B. A social contract   C. Nature   D. Force

---

①According to Rousseau, laws apply to all people as a whole and they reflect the general will. A declaration of the sovereign that applies to only certain subjects is not a law, but a decree. Ideally, laws must be agreed upon and passed by the people as a whole.

②In a healthy republic, Rousseau defined the sovereign as all the citizens acting collectively. Together, they voice the general will and the laws of the state. The sovereign cannot be represented, divided, or broken up in any way: only all the people speaking collectively can be sovereign.

③Magistracy: local administrational order.

④Rousseau makes a critical distinction between what truly constitutes the will of a group of people. While the general will looks out for the common good, the will of all looks out for private interests and is simply the sum of these competing interests.

2. "Man is born free and everywhere he is in _____."
A. fetters   B. shackles   C. handcuffs   D. chains

3. Which of the following is NOT a term Rousseau uses to describe a political association formed by a legitimate social contract?
A. Republic   B. Sovereign
C. Monarchy   D. Body politic

4. Which of the following is NOT a term Rousseau uses to describe the members of a political association formed by a legitimate social contract?
A. Citizens   B. Serfs   C. Subjects   D. A people

5. The Social Contract discusses the _____.
A. Mayflower Compact   B. Magna Carta
C. public will   D. general will

Ⅲ. **Translate the following paragraph (in *The Social Contract*) which describes the essence of the social contract.**

Only when the voice of duty takes the place of physical impulses and right of appetite, does man, who so far had considered only himself, find that he is forced to act on different principles, and to consult his reason before listening to his inclinations. Although, in this state, he deprives himself of some advantages which he got from nature, he gains in return others so great, his faculties are so stimulated and developed, his ideas so extended, his feelings so ennobled, and his whole soul so uplifted.

Ⅳ. **Discuss the following questions with groups.**

1. Everything in Tao Yuanming's poems is from very common daily life but contains the poet's life ideals. Can you illustrate this with some examples in his "Back to Pastoral Life"?

2. "The Peach Blossom Spring" is Tao Yuanming's version of the West's Utopia, or Garden of Eden before the snake entered the picture. What are the characteristics of Utopia? What is Utopian Literature in Chinese and Western culture?

3. Read the following two poems and discuss their similarities and differences in terms of the description of nature.

Daffodils

by William Wordsworth

I wandered lonely as a cloud
That floats on high o'er vales and hills,
When all at once I saw a crowd,
A host, of golden daffodils;
Beside the lake, beneath the trees,

Fluttering and dancing in the breeze.

Continuous as the stars that shine
And twinkle on the Milky Way,
They stretched in never-ending line
Along the margin of a bay:
Ten thousand saw I at a glance,
Tossing their heads in sprightly dance.

The waves beside them danced, but they
Out-did the sparkling waves in glee:
A Poet could not but be gay,
In such a jocund company:
I gazed—and gazed—but little thought
What wealth the show to me had brought:

For oft, when on my couch I lie
In vacant or in pensive mood,
They flash upon that inward eye
Which is the bliss of solitude;
And then my heart with pleasure fills,
And dances with the daffodils.

饮酒：其五

陶渊明

结庐在人境，而无车马喧。
问君何能尔？心远地自偏。
采菊东篱下，悠然见南山。
山气日夕佳，飞鸟相与还。
此中有真意，欲辨已忘言。

4. What is the social contract? Why do we agree to social contract?

5. Rousseau believed that the family itself is maintained only by convention, and the children remain attached to the father only so long as they need him for their preservation. Do you agree? According to Rousseau, the family may be called the first model of political societies: the ruler corresponds to the father, and the people to the children, do you know any similar interpretation in Chinese culture?

Session Three (Extensive Reading)   A Modest Proposal①

Jonathan Swift②

ABOUT THE AUTHOR

It is a melancholy object to those, who walk through this great town, or travel in the country, when they see the streets, the roads and cabbin-doors crowded with beggars of the female sex, followed by three, four, or six children, all in rags, and importuning every passenger for an alms. These mothers instead of being able to work for their honest livelihood, are forced to employ all their time in stroling to beg sustenance for their helpless infants who, as they grow up, either turn thieves for want of work, or leave their dear native country, to fight for the Pretender in Spain, or sell themselves to the Barbadoes.

I think it is agreed by all parties, that this prodigious number of children in the arms, or on the backs, or at the heels of their mothers, and frequently of their fathers, is in the present deplorable state of the kingdom, a very great additional grievance; and therefore whoever could find out a fair, cheap and easy method of making these children sound and useful members of the common-wealth, would deserve so well of the publick, as to have his statue set up for a preserver of the nation.

But my intention is very far from being confined to provide only for the children of professed beggars: it is of a much greater extent, and shall take in the whole number of infants at a certain age, who are born of parents in effect as little able to support them, as those who demand our charity in the streets.

As to my own part, having turned my thoughts for many years, upon this important subject, and maturely weighed the several schemes of our projectors, I have always found them grossly mistaken in their computation. It is true, a child just dropt from its dam, may be supported by her milk, for a solar year, with little other nourishment: at most not above the value of two shillings, which the mother may certainly get, or the value in scraps, by

---

①Excerpts from the essay "A Modest Proposal for Preventing the Children of Poor People From being a Burthen to their Parents or Country and for Making them Beneficial to the Public." Using irony and hyperbole, the essay mocks heartless attitudes toward the poor among English and Irish elites by proposing that impoverished families sell their infant children to be killed and eaten by the rich.

②Jonathan Swift (1667A.D.-1745A.D.) was an Anglo-Irish priest, essayist, political writer and poet, considered the foremost satirist in the English language. Swift's fiercely ironic novels and essays, including world classics such as *Gulliver's Travels* and *The Tale of the Tub*, were immensely popular in his own time for their ribald humor and imaginative insight into human nature. Swift's object was to expose corruption and express political and social criticism through indirection.

her lawful occupation of begging; and it is exactly at one year old that I propose to provide for them in such a manner, as, instead of being a charge upon their parents, or the parish, or wanting food and raiment for the rest of their lives, they shall, on the contrary, contribute to the feeding, and partly to the cloathing of many thousands.

There is likewise another great advantage in my scheme, that it will prevent those voluntary abortions, and that horrid practice of women murdering their bastard children, alas! too frequent among us, sacrificing the poor innocent babes, I doubt, more to avoid the expence than the shame, which would move tears and pity in the most savage and inhuman breast.

The number of souls in this kingdom being usually reckoned one million and a half, of these I calculate there may be about two hundred thousand couple whose wives are breeders; from which number I subtract thirty thousand couple, who are able to maintain their own children, (although I apprehend there cannot be so many, under the present distresses of the kingdom) but this being granted, there will remain an hundred and seventy thousand breeders. I again subtract fifty thousand, for those women who miscarry, or whose children die by accident or disease within the year. There only remain an hundred and twenty thousand children of poor parents annually born. The question therefore is, How this number shall be reared, and provided for? which, as I have already said, under the present situation of affairs, is utterly impossible by all the methods hitherto proposed. For we can neither employ them in handicraft or agriculture; we neither build houses, (I mean in the country) nor cultivate land: they can very seldom pick up a livelihood by stealing till they arrive at six years old; except where they are of towardly parts, although I confess they learn the rudiments much earlier; during which time they can however be properly looked upon only as probationers: As I have been informed by a principal gentleman in the county of Cavan, who protested to me, that he never knew above one or two instances under the age of six, even in a part of the kingdom so renowned for the quickest proficiency in that art.

I am assured by our merchants, that a boy or a girl before twelve years old, is no saleable commodity, and even when they come to this age, they will not yield above three pounds, or three pounds and half a crown at most, on the exchange; which cannot turn to account either to the parents or kingdom, the charge of nutriments and rags having been at least four times that value.

I shall now therefore humbly propose my own thoughts, which I hope will not be liable to the least objection.

I have been assured by a very knowing American of my acquaintance in London, that a young healthy child well nursed, is, at a year old, a most delicious nourishing and wholesome food, whether stewed, roasted, baked, or boiled; and I make no doubt that it will equally serve in a fricasie, or a ragoust.

I do therefore humbly offer it to publick consideration, that of the hundred and twenty thousand children, already computed, twenty thousand may be reserved for breed, whereof only one fourth part to be males; which is more than we allow to sheep, black cattle, or swine, and my reason is, that these children are seldom the fruits of marriage, a circumstance not much regarded by our savages, therefore, one male will be sufficient to serve four females. That the remaining hundred thousand may, at a year old, be offered in sale to the persons of quality and fortune, through the kingdom, always advising the mother to let them suck plentifully in the last month, so as to render them plump, and fat for a good table. A child will make two dishes at an entertainment for friends, and when the family dines alone, the fore or hind quarter will make a reasonable dish, and seasoned with a little pepper or salt, will be very good boiled on the fourth day, especially in winter.

I have reckoned upon a medium, that a child just born will weigh 12 pounds, and in a solar year, if tolerably nursed, encreaseth to 28 pounds.

I grant this food will be somewhat dear, and therefore very proper for landlords, who, as they have already devoured most of the parents, seem to have the best title to the children.

Infant's flesh will be in season throughout the year, but more plentiful in March, and a little before and after; for we are told by a grave author, an eminent French physician, that fish being a prolifick dyet, there are more children born in Roman Catholick countries about nine months after Lent, the markets will be more glutted than usual, because the number of Popish infants, is at least three to one in this kingdom, and therefore it will have one other collateral advantage, by lessening the number of Papists among us.

I have already computed the charge of nursing a beggar's child (in which list I reckon all cottagers, labourers, and four-fifths of the farmers) to be about two shillings per annum, rags included; and I believe no gentleman would repine to give ten shillings for the carcass of a good fat child, which, as I have said, will make four dishes of excellent nutritive meat, when he hath only some particular friend, or his own family to dine with him. Thus the squire will learn to be a good landlord, and grow popular among his tenants, the mother will have eight shillings neat profit, and be fit for work till she produces another child.

Those who are more thrifty (as I must confess the times require) may flea the carcass; the skin of which, artificially dressed, will make admirable gloves for ladies, and summer boots for fine gentlemen.

As to our City of Dublin, shambles may be appointed for this purpose, in the most convenient parts of it, and butchers we may be assured will not be wanting; although I rather recommend buying the children alive, and dressing them hot from the knife, as we do roasting pigs.

A very worthy person, a true lover of his country, and whose virtues I highly esteem, was lately pleased in discoursing on this matter, to offer a refinement upon my scheme. He said, that many gentlemen of this kingdom, having of late destroyed their deer, he conceived that the want of venison might be well supplied by the bodies of young lads and maidens, not exceeding fourteen years of age, nor under twelve; so great a number of both sexes in every county being now ready to starve for want of work and service: and these to be disposed of by their parents if alive, or otherwise by their nearest relations. But with due deference to so excellent a friend, and so deserving a patriot, I cannot be altogether in his sentiments; for as to the males, my American acquaintance assured me from frequent experience, that their flesh was generally tough and lean, like that of our schoolboys, by continual exercise, and their taste disagreeable, and to fatten them would not answer the charge. Then as to the females, it would, I think, with humble submission, be a loss to the publick, because they soon would become breeders themselves: and besides, it is not improbable that some scrupulous people might be apt to censure such a practice, (although indeed very unjustly) as a little bordering upon cruelty, which, I confess, hath always been with me the strongest objection against any project, how well soever intended.

Unit Three   Nature

寄蜉蝣于天地,渺沧海之一粟。哀吾生之须臾,羡长江之无穷;挟飞仙以遨游,抱明月而长终。知不可乎骤得,托遗响于悲风。

——苏轼(中国文学家、诗人、书法家)

Mayflies visiting between heaven and earth, infinitesimal grains in the vast sea, mourning the passing of our instant of life, envying the long river which never ends. Let me cling to a flying immortal and roam far off, and live forever with the full moon in my arms. But knowing that this art is not easily learned, I commit the fading echoes to the sad wind.
—Su Shi(Chinese essayist, poet, and calligrapher)

We need the tonic of wildness, —to wade sometimes in marshes where the bittern and the meadow-hen lurk, and hear the booming of the snipe; to smell the whispering sedge where only some wilder and more solitary fowl builds her nest, and the mink crawls with its belly close to the ground. At the same time that we are earnest to explore and learn all things, we require that all things be mysterious and unexplorable, that land and sea be infinitely wild, unsurveyed and unfathomed by us because unfathomable.
—Henry David Thoreau(American naturalist, essayist, and philosopher)

Session One
The First Ode to the Red Cliff (Qian Chi Bi Fu)

Su Shi

ABOUT THE AUTHOR

Su Shi (1037A.D.-1101A.D.), also known as Su Dongpo, was one of Chinese greatest poets and essayists, who was also an accomplished calligrapher and a public official.

A member of a literary family, the young Su Shi performed brilliantly in his official examinations and was rewarded with the first of the many official positions he occupied during his long and distinguished career. While Su was popular with the people of the various provinces in which he industriously served, he sometimes encountered criticism from the frequently changing heads of state. Wang Anshi[①], prime minister under the Song emperor Shenzong and an accomplished poet himself, banished Su to Huangzhou, Hubei province, in 1079, because of Su's opposition to some of Wang's radical reform measures. Despite his five-year banishment, Su remained friendly toward Wang, later exchanging poems with him. He demonstrated this same optimism and lack of bitterness when he was banished by other forces to Hainan Island in 1094. Shortly before his death he was allowed to return to the mainland and was restored to favour and office.

Su was a master of nearly all literary forms, including shi (regulated verse), the ci song form, fu (prose poetry), and essays, as well as calligraphy and painting. Emphasizing spontaneity and expressiveness, he made significant efforts to loosen poetic conventions on form and content, especially in ci, and became known as the founder of the haofang ("heroic abandon") school of writing. The optimism Su demonstrated in his private and political life can be seen also in his poems, many of which vividly describe his own experiences.

ABOUT "THE FIRST ODE TO THERED CLIFF"

In 1079 Su was falsely accused in Wutai Poem Incident[②] and exiled to Huangzhou (黄州). This marked a turning point in his life. While he experienced great hardship in life, most of his great literary achievements were composed around this time.

---

①Wang Anshi (1021A.D. - 1086A.D.) was a Chinese economist, philosopher, poet, and politician during the Song dynasty. He served as chancellor and attempted major and controversial socioeconomic reforms known as the New Policies. These reforms constituted the core concepts of the Song-Dynasty Reformists, in contrast to their rivals, the Conservatives, led by the Chancellor Sima Guang.

②乌台诗案。

The "First Ode on the Red Cliffs"①, written in 1082, is a piece of writing in the fu form. It describes a trip that Su Shi took with his friends on the Yangtze River, which took them past the purported site of the Battle of Red Cliffs.

On the boat trip Su Shi sang a song and one of his friends accompanied him with a xiao, a traditional Chinese flute. The tune was sad, so the author asked why. The guest said that the place reminded him of Cao Cao②, who had been a hero of an era, but was no longer there. This made him realize the insignificance of human beings in comparison to the river and universe. Su Shi, however, considered the matter from a relativism aspect that both an individual and nature can be constantly changeable or immortal. He also pointed out that everything has its own owner, so one should not take what does not belong to him/her, except those eternal treasures of the creator like the moon or wind which everyone can enjoy. The guest was delighted at last and fell asleep along with the author.

READING

前赤壁赋

壬戌之秋，七月既望③，苏子与客泛舟游于赤壁之下。清风徐来，水波不兴。举酒属客，诵明月之诗，歌窈窕之章。少焉，月出于东山之上，徘徊于斗牛之间④。白露横江，水光接天。纵一苇之所如，凌万顷之茫然。浩浩乎如冯虚御风，而不知其所止⑤；飘飘乎如遗世独立，羽化而登仙⑥。

于是饮酒乐甚，扣舷而歌之。歌曰："桂棹兮兰桨，击空明兮溯流光。渺渺兮予怀，望美人兮天一方。"客有吹洞箫者，倚歌而和之。其声呜呜然，如怨如慕，如泣如诉⑦；余音袅袅，不绝

---

①《前赤壁赋》。

②Cao Cao (155A.D.-220A.D.) was a Chinese poet, statesman, and warlord. He was the penultimate grand chancellor of the Eastern Han dynasty who rose to great power in the final years of the dynasty. As one of the central figures of the Three Kingdoms period, he laid the foundations for what was to become the state of Cao Wei and was posthumously honoured as "Emperor Wu of Wei" although he never officially claimed the title Emperor of China or proclaimed himself "Son of Heaven" during his lifetime. He remains a controversial historical figure, and is often portrayed as a cruel and merciless tyrant in subsequent literature; however, he has also been praised as a brilliant ruler, military genius, and great poet with unrivalled charisma who treated his subordinates like his family.

③"七月既望": the sixteenth day of the seventh month.

④"月出于东山之上，徘徊于斗牛之间": after a while the moon came up above the hills to the east, and wandered between the Dipper and the Herdboy Star.

⑤"浩浩乎如冯虚御风，而不知其所止": as though we were leaning on the void with the winds for chariot, on a journey none knew where.

⑥"飘飘乎如遗世独立，羽化而登仙": hovering above as though we had left the world of men behind us and risen as immortals on newly sprouted wings.

⑦"如怨如慕，如泣如诉": the notes were like sobs, as though he were complaining, longing, weeping, accusing.

如缕。舞幽壑之潜蛟,泣孤舟之嫠妇①。

苏子愀然,正襟危坐,而问客曰:"何为其然也?"客曰:"'月明星稀,乌鹊南飞。'此非曹孟德之诗乎?西望夏口,东望武昌,山川相缪,郁乎苍苍,此非孟德之困于周郎②者乎?方其破荆州,下江陵,顺流而东也,舳舻千里,旌旗蔽空③,酾酒临江,横槊赋诗,固一世之雄也,而今安在哉?况吾与子渔樵于江渚之上,侣鱼虾而友麋鹿④,驾一叶之扁舟,举匏樽以相属⑤;寄蜉蝣与天地,渺沧海之一粟⑥。哀吾生之须臾,羡长江之无穷。挟飞仙以遨游,抱明月而长终。知不可乎骤得,托遗响于悲风。"

苏子曰:"客亦知夫水与月乎?逝者如斯,而未尝往也⑦;盈虚者如彼,而卒莫消长也⑧。盖将自其变者而观之,而天地曾不能一瞬;自其不变者而观之,则物与我皆无尽也,而又何羡乎?且夫天地之间,物各有主,苟非吾之所有,虽一毫而莫取。惟江上之清风,与山间之明月,耳得之而为声,目遇之而成色,取之无禁,用之不竭。是造物者之无尽藏也,而吾与子之所共适。"

客喜而笑,洗盏更酌。肴核既尽,杯盘狼藉。相与枕藉乎舟中,不知东方之既白。

Session Two *Walden*

Henry David Thoreau

ABOUT THE AUTHOR

Henry David Thoreau (1817A.D.-1862A.D.) was an American philosopher, poet, and environmental scientist. He was born on July 12, 1817, in Concord, Massachusetts, to John and Cynthia Dunbar Thoreau. He had two older siblings, Helen and John, and a younger

---

①"余音袅袅,不绝如缕;舞幽壑之潜蛟,泣孤舟之嫠妇": the wavering resonance lingered, a thread of sound which did not snap off, till the dragons underwater danced in the black depths, and a widow wept in our lonely boat.

②"周郎": Zhou Yu (175A.D.-210A.D.) was a Chinese military general and strategist serving under the warlord Sun Ce in the late Eastern Han dynasty of China. After Sun Ce died in the year 200, he continued serving under Sun Quan, Sun Ce's younger brother and successor. Zhou Yu is primarily known for his leading role in defeating the numerically superior forces of the northern warlord Cao Cao at the Battle of Red Cliffs in late 208, and again at the Battle of Jiangling in 209.

③"舳舻千里,旌旗蔽空": his vessels were prow by stern for a thousand miles, his banners hid the sky.

④"渔樵于江渚之上,侣鱼虾而友麋鹿": fishermen and woodcutters on the river's isles, with fish and shrimp and deer for mates.

⑤"驾一叶之扁舟,举匏樽以相属": riding a boat as shallow as a leaf, pouring each other drinks from bottle gourds.

⑥"寄蜉蝣与天地,渺沧海之一粟": mayflies visiting between heaven and earth, infinitesimal grains in the vast sea.

⑦"逝者如斯,而未尝往也": the water streams past so swiftly yet is never gone.

⑧"盈虚者如彼,而卒莫消长也": the moon for ever waxes and wanes yet finally has never grown nor diminished.

sister, Sophia. The family moved to Chelmsford in 1818, to Boston in 1821, and back to Concord in 1823. Thoreau had two educations in Concord. The first occurred through his explorations of the local environment, which were encouraged by his mother's interest in nature. The second was his preparation at Concord Academy for study at Harvard University. He entered Harvard in 1833 and graduated in 1837. The year he graduated he began the journal that was a primary source for his lectures and published work throughout his life.

Henry David Thoreau is recognized as an important contributor to the American literary and philosophical movement known as New England Transcendentalism①. His essays, books and poems weave together two central themes over the course of his intellectual career: nature and the conduct of life. The continuing importance of these two themes is well illustrated by the fact that the last two essays Thoreau published during his lifetime were "The Last Days of John Brown" and "The Succession of Forest Trees" (both in 1860). In his moral and political work Thoreau aligned himself with the post-Socratic schools of Greek philosophy—in particular, the Cynics and the Stoics②—that used philosophy as a means of addressing ordinary human experience. His naturalistic writing integrated straightforward observation and cataloguing with transcendentalist interpretations of nature and the wilderness. In many of his works Thoreau brought these interpretations of nature to bear on how people live or ought to live.

Thoreau's importance as a philosophical writer was little appreciated during his lifetime, but his two most noted works, *Walden; or, Life in the Woods* (1854) and *Resistance to Civil Government*③ (1849), gradually developed a following, and by the latter half of the 20th

---

① Transcendentalism is a philosophical movement that developed in the late 1820s and 1830s in New England. A core belief is in the inherent goodness of people and nature, and while society and its institutions have corrupted the purity of the individual, people are at their best when truly "self-reliant" and independent. Transcendentalists saw divine experience inherent in the everyday, rather than believing in a distant heaven. Transcendentalists saw physical and spiritual phenomena as part of dynamic processes rather than discrete entities. Transcendentalism emphasizes subjective intuition over objective empiricism. Adherents believe that individuals are capable of generating completely original insights with little attention and deference to past masters. It arose as a reaction, to protest against the general state of intellectualism and spirituality at the time.

② The Stoics are especially known for teaching that "virtue is the only good" for human beings, and those external things—such as health, wealth, and pleasure—are not good nor bad in themselves but have value as "material for virtue to act upon." The Stoics also held that certain destructive emotions resulted from errors of judgment, and they believed people should aim to maintain a will that is "in accordance with nature". Because of this, the Stoics thought the best indication of an individual's philosophy was not what a person said but how a person behaved. To live a good life, one had to understand the rules of the natural order since they thought everything was rooted in nature.

③ *Resistance to Civil Government*, also called On the Duty of Civil Disobedience or Civil Disobedience for short, is an essay by American transcendentalist Henry David Thoreau that was first published in 1849. In it, Thoreau argues that individuals should not permit governments to overrule or atrophy their consciences, and that they have a duty to avoid allowing such acquiescence to enable the government to make them the agents of injustice. Thoreau was motivated in part by his disgust with slavery and the Mexican-American War (1846–1848).

century, had become classic texts in American thought. Not only have these texts been used widely to address issues in political philosophy, moral theory, and, more recently, environmentalism, but they have also been of central importance to those who see philosophy as an engagement with ordinary experience and not as an abstract deductive exercise. In this vein, Thoreau's work has been recognized as having foreshadowed central insights of later philosophical movements such as existentialism① and pragmatism②.

Toward the end of his life Thoreau's naturalistic interests took a more scientific turn; he pursued a close examination of local fauna ③ and kept detailed records of his observations. Nevertheless, he kept one eye on the moral and political developments of his time, often expressing his positions with rhetorical fire as in his "A Plea for Captain John Brown" (1860). He achieved an elegant integration of his naturalism and his moral interests in several late essays that were published posthumously, among them "Walking" and "Wild Apples" (both in 1862).

ABOUT *WALDEN*

Walden, in full *Walden; or, Life in the Woods*, a series of 18 essays by Henry David Thoreau, was published in 1854. An important contribution to New England Transcendentalism, the book was a record of Thoreau's experiment in simple living on the northern shore of Walden Pond in eastern Massachusetts (1845 – 1847). *Walden* is viewed not only as a philosophical treatise on labour, leisure, self-reliance, and individualism but also as an influential piece of nature writing. It is considered Thoreau's masterwork.

Walden is the product of the two years and two months Thoreau lived in semi-isolation by Walden Pond near Concord, Massachusetts. He built a small cabin on land owned by his friend Ralph Waldo Emerson ④ and was almost totally self-sufficient, growing his own

---

①Existentialism is a form of philosophical inquiry that explores the problem of human existence and centers on the experience of thinking, feeling, and acting. In the view of the existentialist, the individual's starting point has been called "the existential angst", a sense of dread, disorientation, confusion, or anxiety in the face of an apparently meaningless or absurd world. Existentialist thinkers frequently explore issues related to the meaning, purpose, and value of human existence.

②Pragmatism is a philosophical tradition that considers words and thought as tools and instruments for prediction, problem solving, and action, and rejects the idea that the function of thought is to describe, represent, or mirror reality. Pragmatists contend that most philosophical topics—such as the nature of knowledge, language, concepts, meaning, belief, and science—are all best viewed in terms of their practical uses and successes.

③Local fauna is the animal life, especially the animals characteristic of a region, period, or special environment.

④Ralph Waldo Emerson (1803A.D.-1882A.D.) American essayist, lecturer, philosopher, abolitionist, and poet who led the transcendentalist movement of the mid-19th century. He was seen as a champion of individualism and a prescient critic of the countervailing pressures of society, and his ideology was disseminated through dozens of published essays and more than 1,500 public lectures across the United States.

vegetables and doing odd jobs. It was his intention at Walden Pond to live simply and have time to contemplate, walk in the woods, write, and commune with nature. As he explained, "I went to the woods because I wished to live deliberately, to front only the essential facts of life." The resulting book is a series of essays, or meditations, beginning with "Economy", in which he discussed his experiment and included a detailed account of the construction (and cost) of his cabin. Thoreau extolled the benefits of literature in "Reading", though in the following essay, "Sounds", he noted the limits of books and implored the reader to live mindfully, "being forever on the alert" to the sounds and sights in his or her own life. "Solitude" praised the friendliness of nature, which made the "fancied advantages of human neighbourhood insignificant." Later essays included "Visitors", "Higher Laws", "Winter Animals", and "Spring".

Relatively neglected during Thoreau's lifetime, *Walden* achieved tremendous popularity in the 20th century. Thoreau's description of the physical act of living day by day at Walden Pond gave the book authority, while his command of a clear, straightforward, but elegant style helped raise it to the level of a literary classic. Oft-repeated quotes from *Walden* include: "The mass of men lead lives of quiet desperation"; "Beware of all enterprises that require new clothes"; and "If a man does not keep pace with his companions, perhaps it is because he hears a different drummer."

READING

Chapter 17 Spring

One attraction in coming to the woods to live was that I should have leisure and opportunity to see the spring come in. The ice in the pond at length begins to be honey-combed, and I can set my heel in it as I walk. Fogs and rains and warmer suns are gradually melting the snow; the days have grown sensibly longer; and I see how I shall get through the winter without adding to my woodpile, for large fires are no longer necessary. I am on the alert for the first signs of spring, to hear the chance note of some arriving bird, or the striped squirrel's chirp, for his stores must be now nearly exhausted, or see the woodchuck venture out of his winter quarters. On the 13th of March, after I had heard the bluebird, song-sparrow, and red-wing, the ice was still nearly a foot thick. As the weather grew warmer it was not sensibly worn away by the water, nor broken up and floated off as in rivers, but, though it was completely melted for half a rod in width about the shore, the middle was merely honey-combed and saturated with water, so that you could put your foot through it when six inches thick; but by the next day evening, perhaps, after a warm rain followed by fog, it would have wholly disappeared, all gone off with the fog, spirited away. One year I went across the middle only five days before it disappeared entirely. In 1845 Walden was first completely open on the 1st of April; in '46, the 25th of March; in '47, the

8th of April; in '51, the 28th of March; in '52, the 18th of April; in '53, the 23d of March; in '54, about the 7th of April.

Every incident connected with the breaking up of the rivers and ponds and the settling of the weather is particularly interesting to us who live in a climate of so great extremes. When the warmer days come, they who dwell near the river hear the ice crack at night with a startling whoop as loud as artillery①, as if its icy fetters were rent from end to end, and within a few days see it rapidly going out. So the alligator comes out of the mud with quakings of the earth. One old man, who has been a close observer of Nature, and seems as thoroughly wise in regard to all her operations as if she had been put upon the stocks when he was a boy, and he had helped to lay her keel,—who has come to his growth, and can hardly acquire more of natural lore if he should live to the age of Methuselah②,—told me, and I was surprised to hear him express wonder at any of Nature's operations, for I thought that there were no secrets between them, that one spring day he took his gun and boat, and thought that he would have a little sport with the ducks. There was ice still on the meadows, but it was all gone out of the river, and he dropped down without obstruction from Sudbury, where he lived, to Fair-Haven Pond, which he found, unexpectedly, covered for the most part with a firm field of ice. It was a warm day, and he was surprised to see so great a body of ice remaining. Not seeing any ducks, he hid his boat on the north or back side of an island in the pond, and then concealed himself in the bushes on the south side, to await them. The ice was melted for three or four rods from the shore, and there was a smooth and warm sheet of water, with a muddy bottom, such as the ducks love, within, and he thought it likely that some would be along pretty soon. After he had lain still there about an hour he heard a low and seemingly very distant sound, but singularly grand and impressive, unlike anything he had ever heard, gradually swelling and increasing as if it would have a universal and memorable ending, a sullen rush and roar, which seemed to him all at once like the sound of a vast body of fowl coming in to settle there, and, seizing his gun, he started up in haste and excited; but he found, to his surprise, that the whole body of the ice had started while he lay there, and drifted in to the shore, and the sound he had heard was made by its edge grating on the shore,—at first gently nibbled and crumbled off, but at length heaving up and scattering its wrecks along the island to a considerable height before it came to a standstill.

At length the sun's rays have attained the right angle, and warm winds blow up mist and rain and melt the snow banks, and the sun dispersing the mist smiles on a checkered landscape of russet③ and white smoking with incense, through which the traveler picks his

---

①Artillery: weapons (such as bows, slings, and catapults) for discharging missiles.

②Methuselah was a biblical patriarch and a figure in Judaism, Christianity and Islam. His was the longest human lifespan of all those given in the Bible, 969 years.

③Russet: a reddish brown.

way from islet to islet①, cheered by the music of a thousand tinkling rills② and rivulets whose veins are filled with the blood of winter which they are bearing off.

Few phenomena gave me more delight than to observe the forms which thawing sand and clay assume in flowing down the sides of a deep cut on the railroad through which I passed on my way to the village, a phenomenon not very common on so large a scale, though the number of freshly exposed banks of the right material must have been greatly multiplied since railroads were invented. The material was sand of every degree of fineness and of various rich colors, commonly mixed with a little clay. When the frost comes out in the spring, and even in a thawing day in the winter, the sand begins to flow down the slopes like lava③, sometimes bursting out through the snow and overflowing it where no sand was to be seen before. Innumerable little streams overlap and interlace one with another, exhibiting a sort of hybrid product, which obeys halfway the law of currents, and halfway that of vegetation. As it flows it takes the forms of sappy leaves or vines, making heaps of pulpy sprays a foot or more in depth, and resembling, as you look down on them, the laciniated④, lobed, and imbricated thalluses⑤ of some lichens; or you are reminded of coral, of leopard's paws or birds' feet, of brains or lungs or bowels, and excrements of all kinds. It is a truly grotesque vegetation, whose forms and color we see imitated in bronze, a sort of architectural foliage more ancient and typical than acanthus, chiccory, ivy, vine, or any vegetable leaves; destined perhaps, under some circumstances, to become a puzzle to future geologists. The whole cut impressed me as if it were a cave with its stalactites⑥ laid open to the light. The various shades of the sand are singularly rich and agreeable, embracing the different iron colors, brown, gray, yellowish, and reddish. When the flowing mass reaches the drain at the foot of the bank it spreads out flatter into strands, the separate streams losing their semi-cylindrical form and gradually becoming more flat and broad, running together as they are more moist, till they form an almost flat sand, still variously and beautifully shaded, but in which you can trace the original forms of vegetation; till at length, in the water itself, they are converted into banks, like those formed off the mouths of rivers, and the forms of vegetation are lost in the ripple marks on the bottom.

The whole bank, which is from twenty to forty feet high, is sometimes overlaid with a mass of this kind of foliage, or sandy rupture, for a quarter of a mile on one or both sides,

---

①Islet: a little island.

②Rill: a very small brook.

③Lava: molten rock that issues from a volcano or from a fissure in the surface of a planet (such as earth) or moon.

④Laciniate: cut into narrow, irregular lobes; slashed; jagged.

⑤Thallus: a simple vegetative body undifferentiated into true leaves, stem, and root, ranging from an aggregation of filaments to a complex plantlike form.

⑥Stalactite: a deposit of calcium carbonate (such as calcite) resembling an icicle hanging from the roof or sides of a cave.

the produce of one spring day. What makes this sand foliage remarkable is its springing into existence thus suddenly. When I see on the one side the inert bank,—for the sun acts on one side first,—and on the other this luxuriant foliage, the creation of an hour, I am affected as if in a peculiar sense I stood in the laboratory of the Artist who made the world and me,— had come to where he was still at work, sporting on this bank, and with excess of energy strewing his fresh designs about. I feel as if I were nearer to the vitals① of the globe, for this sandy overflow is something such a foliaceous mass as the vitals of the animal body. You find thus in the very sands an anticipation of the vegetable leaf. No wonder that the earth expresses itself outwardly in leaves, it so labors with the idea inwardly. The atoms have already learned this law, and are pregnant by it. The overhanging leaf sees here its prototype②. Internally, whether in the globe or animal body, it is a moist thick lobe, a word especially applicable to the liver and lungs and the leaves of fat, (λείβω, labor, lapsus, to flow or slip downward, a lapsing; λοβος, globus, lobe, globe; also lap, flap, and many other words,) externally a dry thin leaf, even as the f and v are a pressed and dried b. The radicals of lobe are lb, the soft mass of the b (single lobed, or B, double lobed,) with the liquid l behind it pressing it forward. In globe, glb, the guttural g adds to the meaning the capacity of the throat. The feathers and wings of birds are still drier and thinner leaves. Thus, also, you pass from the lumpish grub in the earth to the airy and fluttering butterfly. The very globe continually transcends and translates itself, and becomes winged in its orbit. Even ice begins with delicate crystal leaves, as if it had flowed into moulds which the fronds of water plants have impressed on the watery mirror. The whole tree itself is but one leaf, and rivers are still vaster leaves whose pulp is intervening earth, and towns and cities are the ova of insects in their axils.

When the sun withdraws the sand ceases to flow, but in the morning the streams will start once more and branch and branch again into a myriad of others. You here see perchance how blood vessels are formed. If you look closely you observe that first there pushes forward from the thawing mass a stream of softened sand with a drop-like point, like the ball of the finger, feeling its way slowly and blindly downward, until at last with more heat and moisture, as the sun gets higher, the most fluid portion, in its effort to obey the law to which the most inert also yields, separates from the latter and forms for itself a meandering channel or artery within that, in which is seen a little silvery stream glancing like lightning from one stage of pulpy leaves or branches to another, and ever and anon swallowed up in the sand. It is wonderful how rapidly yet perfectly the sand organizes itself as it flows, using the best material its mass affords to form the sharp edges of its channel. Such are the sources of rivers. In the silicious matter which the water deposits is perhaps the bony system, and in the still finer soil and organic matter the fleshy fibre or cellular tissue. What

---

①Vitals: internal bodily organs (such as the heart, lungs and brain) that are essential to life.
②Prototype: an original model on which something is patterned.

is man but a mass of thawing clay? The ball of the human finger is but a drop congealed. The fingers and toes flow to their extent from the thawing mass of the body. Who knows what the human body would expand and flow out to under a more genial heaven? Is not the hand a spreadingpalm leaf with its lobes and veins? The ear may be regarded, fancifully, as a lichen, umbilicaria, on the side of the head, with its lobe or drop. The lip—labium, from labor (?)—laps or lapses from the sides of the cavernous mouth. The nose is a manifest congealed drop or stalactite. The chin is a still larger drop, the confluent dripping of the face. The cheeks are a slide from the brows into the valley of the face, opposed and diffused by the cheek bones. Each rounded lobe of the vegetable leaf, too, is a thick and now loitering drop, larger or smaller; the lobes are the fingers of the leaf; and as many lobes as it has, in so many directions it tends to flow, and more heat or other genial influences would have caused it to flow yet farther.

Thus it seemed that this one hillside illustrated the principle of all the operations of Nature. The Maker of this earth but patented a leaf. What Champollion① will decipher this hieroglyphic for us, that we may turn over a new leaf at last? This phenomenon is more exhilarating to me than the luxuriance and fertility of vineyards. True, it is somewhat excrementitious② in its character, and there is no end to the heaps of liver lights and bowels, as if the globe were turned wrong side outward; but this suggests at least that Nature has some bowels, and there again is mother of humanity. This is the frost coming out of the ground; this is Spring. It precedes the green and flowery spring, as mythology precedes regular poetry. I know of nothing more purgative of winter fumes and indigestions. It convinces me that Earth is still in her swaddling clothes, and stretches forth baby fingers on every side. Fresh curls spring from the baldest brow. There is nothing inorganic. These foliaceous heaps lie along the bank like the slag of a furnace, showing that Nature is "in full blast" within. The earth is not a mere fragment of dead history, stratum upon stratum like the leaves of a book, to be studied by geologists and antiquaries chiefly, but living poetry like the leaves of a tree, which precede flowers and fruit,—not a fossil earth, but a living earth; compared with whose great central life all animal and vegetable life is merely parasitic③. Its throes will heave our exuviae④ from their graves. You may melt your metals and cast them into the most beautiful moulds you can; they will never excite me like the forms which this molten earth flows out into. And not only it, but the institutions upon it, are plastic like clay in the hands of the potter.

---

①Jean-François Champollion was a French philologist and orientalist, known primarily as the decipherer of Egyptian hieroglyphs and a founding figure in the field of Egyptology.

②Excrementitious: like waste material, especially fecal matter, that is expelled from the body after digestion.

③Parasitic: living in or on another animal or plant and getting food or protection from it.

④Exuviae: sloughed off natural animal coverings. (such as the skins of snakes)

Ere long, not only on these banks, but on every hill and plain and in every hollow, the frost comes out of the ground like a dormant quadruped from its burrow, and seeks the sea with music, or migrates to other climes in clouds. Thaw with his gentle persuasion is more powerful than Thor with his hammer①. The one melts, the other but breaks in pieces.

When the ground was partially bare of snow, and a few warm days had dried its surface somewhat, it was pleasant to compare the first tender signs of the infant year just peeping forth with the stately beauty of the withered vegetation which had withstood the winter,—life-everlasting, golden-rods, pinweeds, and graceful wild grasses, more obvious and interesting frequently than in summer even, as if their beauty was not ripe till then; even cotton-grass, cat-tails, mulleins, johnswort, hard-hack, meadow-sweet, and other strong stemmed plants, those unexhausted granaries which entertain the earliest birds,—decent weeds, at least, which widowed Nature wears. I am particularly attracted by the arching and sheaf-like top of the wool-grass; it brings back the summer to our winter memories, and is among the forms which art loves to copy, and which, in the vegetable kingdom, have the same relation to types already in the mind of man that astronomy has. It is an antique style older than Greek or Egyptian. Many of the phenomena of Winter are suggestive of an inexpressible tenderness and fragile delicacy. We are accustomed to hear this king described as a rude and boisterous tyrant; but with the gentleness of a lover he adorns the tresses of Summer.

At the approach of spring the red-squirrels got under my house, two at a time, directly under my feet as I sat reading or writing, and kept up the queerest chuckling and chirruping and vocal pirouetting and gurgling sounds that ever were heard; and when I stamped they only chirruped the louder, as if past all fear and respect in their mad pranks, defying humanity to stop them. No you don't—chickaree—chickaree. They were wholly deaf to my arguments, or failed to perceive their force, and fell into a strain of invective② that was irresistible.

The first sparrow of spring! The year beginning with younger hope than ever! The faint silvery warblings heard over the partially bare and moist fields from the blue-bird, the song-sparrow, and the red-wing, as if the last flakes of winter tinkled as they fell! What at such a time are histories, chronologies, traditions, and all written revelations? The brooks sing carols and glees to the spring. The marsh-hawk sailing low over the meadow is already seeking the first slimy life that awakes. The sinking sound of melting snow is heard in all dells, and the ice dissolves apace in the ponds. The grass flames up on the hillsides like a

---

①Thor was one of the most famous and best loved of all the Norse gods. He was the god of thunder and lightning, and he was very strong. Unlike the other gods, Thor travelled from place to place in a chariot pulled by two goats. Although Thor was naturally strong, he wore a special belt, called a girdle, that doubled his strength. But the most important of all of Thor's tools was his hammer.

②Invective: an abusive expression or speech.

spring fire,—"et primitus oritur herba imbribus primoribus evocata,"—as if the earth sent forth an inward heat to greet the returning sun; not yellow but green is the color of its flame;—the symbol of perpetual youth, the grass-blade, like a long green ribbon, streams from the sod into the summer, checked indeed by the frost, but anon pushing on again, lifting its spear of last year's hay with the fresh life below. It grows as steadily as the rill oozes out of the ground. It is almost identical with that, for in the growing days of June, when the rills are dry, the grass blades are their channels, and from year to year the herds drink at this perennial green stream, and the mower draws from it betimes their winter supply. So our human life but dies down to its root, and still puts forth its green blade to eternity.

Walden is melting apace. There is a canal two rods wide along the northerly and westerly sides, and wider still at the east end. A great field of ice has cracked off from the main body. I hear a song-sparrow singing from the bushes on the shore,—olit, olit, olit,—chip, chip, chip, che char,—che wiss, wiss, wiss. He too is helping to crack it. How handsome the great sweeping curves in the edge of the ice, answering somewhat to those of the shore, but more regular! It is unusually hard, owing to the recent severe but transient cold, and all watered or waved like a palace floor. But the wind slides eastward over its opaque surface in vain, till it reaches the living surface beyond. It is glorious to behold this ribbon of water sparkling in the sun, the bare face of the pond full of glee and youth, as if it spoke the joy of the fishes within it, and of the sands on its shore,—a silvery sheen as from the scales of a leuciscus, as it were all one active fish. Such is the contrast between winter and spring. Walden was dead and is alive again. But this spring it broke up more steadily, as I have said.

The change from storm and winter to serene and mild weather, from dark and sluggish hours to bright and elastic ones, is a memorable crisis which all things proclaim. It is seemingly instantaneous at last. Suddenly an influx of light filled my house, though the evening was at hand, and the clouds of winter still overhung it, and the eaves were dripping with sleety rain. I looked out the window, and lo! where yesterday was cold gray ice there lay the transparent pond already calm and full of hope as in a summer evening, reflecting a summer evening sky in its bosom, though none was visible overhead, as if it had intelligence with some remote horizon. I heard a robin in the distance, the first I had heard for many a thousand years, methought, whose note I shall not forget for many a thousand more,—the same sweet and powerful song as of yore. O the evening robin, at the end of a New England summer day! If I could ever find the twig he sits upon! I meanhe; I mean the twig. This at least is not the Turdus migratorius. The pitch-pines and shrub-oaks about my house, which had so long drooped, suddenly resumed their several characters, looked brighter, greener, and more erect and alive, as if effectually cleansed and restored by the rain. I knew that it would not rain any more. You may tell by looking at any twig of the forest, ay, at your very wood-pile, whether its winter is past or not. As it grew darker, I was startled by the honking of geese flying low over the woods, like weary travellers getting in late from southern lakes, and indulging at last in unrestrained complaint and mutual consolation. Standing at my door, I could hear the rush of their wings; when, driving toward my house, they suddenly spied my light, and with hushed clamor wheeled and settled in the pond. So I came in, and shut the door, and passed my first spring night in the woods.

...

COMPREHENSION & EXERCISES

Ⅰ. **Read "Spring" and try to explain the italicized parts in English.**

1. I am on the alert for the first signs of spring, to hear the chance note of some arriving bird, or the striped squirrel's chirp, for his *stores* must be now nearly exhausted, or see the woodchuck venture out of his winter quarters.

2. As the weather grew warmer it was not sensibly worn away by the water, nor broken up and floated off as in rivers, but, though it was completely melted for half a rod in width about the shore, the middle was merely honey-combed and saturated with water, so that you could put your foot through it when six inches thick; but by the next day evening, perhaps, after a warm rain followed by fog, it would have wholly disappeared, all gone off with the fog, *spirited away*.

3. One old man, who has been a close observer of Nature, and seems as thoroughly wise in regard to all her operations as if she had been put upon the stocks when he was a boy, and he had helped to lay her keel,—who has come to his growth, and can hardly acquire more of natural *lore* if he should live to the age of Methuselah…

4. The material was sand of every degree of *fineness* and of various rich colors, commonly mixed with a little clay.

Ⅱ. **Read "The First Ode to the Red Cliff" and "Spring" and answer the questions.**

1. What mood does the party start out with, and why does the musician change the mood so drastically?

2. How does Su Shi restore the mood of the outing?

3. According to Thoreau, what is the major attraction of living the woods?

4. Thoreau call the forms which thawing sand and clay assume "grotesque". Does the writer really find them disgusting, as the word "grotesque" suggests? Why or why not?

5. According to Thoreau, what makes the sand foliage remarkable?

6. In "Spring", Thoreau compares the natural world to human body, can you give any examples? Do you agree with the view that the natural world resembles human body? Why or why not?

7. Thoreau writes "I am affected as if in a peculiar sense I stood in the laboratory of the Artist who made the world and me,—had come to where he was still at work, sporting on this bank, and with excess of energy strewing his fresh designs about." Who do you think the Artist is?

8. Thoreau writes "(the brown and barren spring) precedes the green and flowery spring, as mythology precedes regular poetry." What's your interpretation of the sentence?

9. How natural phenomena are interpreted in "The First Ode to the Red Cliff" and "Spring". Are there any differences between the two ways of interpretations? What are their similarities? Which approach do you prefer?

Ⅲ. **Translate the following paragraph into Chinese.**

The first sparrow of spring! The year beginning with younger hope than ever! The faint silvery warblings heard over the partially bare and moist fields from the blue-bird, the song-sparrow, and the red-wing, as if the last flakes of winter tinkled as they fell! What at such a time are histories, chronologies, traditions, and all written revelations? The brooks sing carols and glees to the spring. The marsh-hawk sailing low over the meadow is already seeking the first slimy life that awakes. The sinking sound of melting snow is heard in all dells, and the ice dissolves apace in the ponds. The grass flames up on the hillsides like a spring fire,—"et primitus oritur herba imbribus primoribus evocata,"—as if the earth sent forth an inward heat to greet the returning sun; not yellow but green is the color of its flame;—the symbol of perpetual youth, the grass-blade, like a long green ribbon, streams from the sod into the summer, checked indeed by the frost, but anon pushing on again, lifting its spear of last year's hay with the fresh life below.

Session Three (Extensive Reading) *Nature*

Ralph Waldo Emerson

To go into solitude, a man needs to retire as much from his chamber as from society. I am not solitary whilst I read and write, though nobody is with me. But if a man would be alone, let him look at the stars. The rays that come from those heavenly worlds, will separate between him and what he touches. One might think the atmosphere was made transparent with this design, to give man, in the heavenly bodies, the perpetual presence of the sublime. Seen in the streets of cities, how great they are! If the stars should appear one night in a thousand years, how would men believe and adore; and preserve for many generations the remembrance of the city of God which had been shown! But every night come out these envoys of beauty, and light the universe with their admonishing smile.

The stars awaken a certain reverence, because though always present, they are inaccessible; but all natural objects make a kindred impression, when the mind is open to their influence. Nature never wears a mean appearance. Neither does the wisest man extort her secret, and lose his curiosity by finding out all her perfection. Nature never became a toy to a wise spirit. The flowers, the animals, the mountains, reflected the wisdom of his best hour, as much as they had delighted the simplicity of his childhood.

When we speak of nature in this manner, we have a distinct but most poetical sense in the mind. We mean the integrity of impression made by manifold natural objects. It is this which distinguishes the stick of timber of the wood-cutter, from the tree of the poet. The charming landscape which I saw this morning, is indubitably made up of some twenty or thirty farms. Miller owns this field, Locke that, and Manning the woodland beyond. But none of them owns the landscape. There is a property in the horizon which no man has but he whose eye can integrate all the parts, that is, the poet. This is the best part of these men's farms, yet to this their warranty-deeds give no title.

To speak truly, few adult persons can see nature. Most persons do not see the sun. At least they have a very superficial seeing. The sun illuminates only the eye of the man, but shines into the eye and the heart of the child. The lover of nature is he whose inward and outward senses are still truly adjusted to each other; who has retained the spirit of infancy even into the era of manhood. His intercourse with heaven and earth, becomes part of his daily food. In the presence of nature, a wild delight runs through the man, in spite of real sorrows. Nature says,—he is my creature, and maugre all his impertinent griefs, he shall be glad with me. Not the sun or the summer alone, but every hour and season yields its tribute of delight; for every hour and change corresponds to and authorizes a different state of the mind, from breathless noon to grimmest midnight. Nature is a setting that fits equally well a comic or a mourning piece. In good health, the air is a cordial of incredible virtue. Crossing a bare common, in snow puddles, at twilight, under a clouded sky, without having in my thoughts any occurrence of special good fortune, I have enjoyed a perfect exhilaration. I am glad to the brink of fear. In the woods too, a man casts off his years, as the snake his slough, and at what period soever of life, is always a child. In the woods, is perpetual youth. Within these plantations of God, a decorum and sanctity reign, a perennial festival is dressed, and the guest sees not how he should tire of them in a thousand years. In the woods, we return to reason and faith. There I feel that nothing can befall me in life,—no disgrace, no calamity, (leaving me my eyes,) which nature cannot repair. Standing on the bare ground,—my head bathed by the blithe air, and uplifted into infinite space,—all mean egotism vanishes. I become a transparent eye-ball; I am nothing; I see all; the currents of the Universal Being circulate through me; I am part or particle of God. The name of the nearest friend sounds then foreign and accidental: to be brothers, to be acquaintances,—master or servant, is then a trifle and a disturbance. I am the lover of uncontained and immortal beauty. In the wilderness, I find something more dear and connate than in streets or villages. In the tranquil landscape, and especially in the distant line of the horizon, man beholds somewhat as beautiful as his own nature.

The greatest delight which the fields and woods minister, is the suggestion of an occult relation between man and the vegetable. I am not alone and unacknowledged. They nod to me, and I to them. The waving of the boughs in the storm, is new to me and old. It takes me by surprise, and yet is not unknown. Its effect is like that of a higher thought or a better emotion coming over me, when I deemed I was thinking justly or doing right.

Yet it is certain that the power to produce this delight, does not reside in nature, but in man, or in a harmony of both. It is necessary to use these pleasures with great temperance. For, nature is not always tricked in holiday attire, but the same scene which yesterday breathed perfume and glittered as for the frolic of the nymphs, is overspread with melancholy today. Nature always wears the colors of the spirit. To a man laboring under calamity, the heat of his own fire hath sadness in it. Then, there is a kind of contempt of the landscape felt by him who has just lost by death a dear friend. The sky is less grand as it shuts down over less worth in the population.

Unit Four Education

三人行,必有我师焉。择其善者而从之,其不善者而改之。

——孔子(中国哲学家、政治家)

If three men are walking together, one of them is bound to be good enough to be my teacher. I will select their good qualities and follow them, their bad qualities and avoid them.

—Confucius(Chinese philosopher and politician)

The understanding is not a vessel which must be filled, but firewood, which needs to be kindled; and love of learning and love of truth are what should kindle it.

—L. Mestrius Plutarchus(Greek writer and philosopher)

Unit Four   Education

Session One   On the Teacher (Shi Shuo)

Han Yu

ABOUT THE AUTHOR

Han Yu (768B.C.-824B.C.), also called Han Changli or Han Wengong, courtesy name Tuizhi, master of Chinese prose, outstanding poet, and the first proponent of what later came to be known as Neo-Confucianism①, which had wide influence in China and Japan. Lived in a time when the Chinese Tang empire (618B.C.-907B.C.) was threatened by military separatism but enjoyed cultural creativity and economic expansion, Han advocated the adoption of guwen, the free, simple prose of these early philosophers, a style unencumbered by the mannerisms and elaborate verselike regularity of the pianwen ("parallel prose") style that was prevalent in Han's time. His own essays (e.g. "On the Way", "On Man", and "On Spirits") are among the most beautiful ever written in Chinese, and they became the most famous models of the prose style he espoused. In his poetry also, Han tried to break out of the existing literary forms, but many of his efforts at literary reform failed. He is considered the first of the renowned "Eight Masters of the Tang and Song." As a thinker, Han's most important idea was that Confucianism is the sole legitimate teaching for human conduct, to the exclusion of Buddhism and Daoism. This was an extreme position in his own time, but it exerted profound influence throughout later Chinese history. Han presented this view most forcefully in his famous essay "Essentials of the Moral Way" (Yuan Dao). This essay asserts that the only Dao is the one based on everyday life, which is the Confucian Way discovered and developed by ancient sage-kings.

---

①Neo-Confucianism emerged during the Tang Dynasty and was influenced by Buddhism and Daoism, despite it rejecting both these religions. Its emergence was largely a response to perceived foreign influences on Chinese politics and thought, and this led the Neo-Confucians, in particular its proponents Han Yu 韩愈 (768B.C.-824B.C.), Li Ao 李翱(772B.C.-841B.C.), and Liu Zongyuan 柳宗元(773B.C.-819B.C.), to challenge the central place of Buddhism. Yu, Ao, and Zongyuan were the earliest Neo-Confucian thinkers who attacked the philosophy of Buddhism and wanted to produce a revival of the Confucian Way. In contrast to the Daoists who stood distant from society, the Neo-Confucians believed that human beings achieved fulfillment by sincere involvement in society. Moreover, the Neo-Confucianists came to disagree with the Buddhists that the world is an illusion as their metaphysics affirmed an ultimate reality.

ABOUT "ON THE TEACHER"①

"On the Teacher" is a treatise on teaching compiled by Han Yu. It was written around 802 and is influenced by the revival of Confucian thought that crystallized during the later half of the Tang period, and of which Han Yu was the most important proponent. In the educational concepts of that time, disciples were required to pose questions to their teacher, and to find out about the true "Way" by a question-and-answer principle. Active instructions by the teacher were not regarded as the principal way of learning. Yet Han Yu was the first who suggested that teachers might lecture their students, instead of having them find the truth by asking questions. His contemporatians therefore harshly criticized him. His book nevertheless broke the path for the emergence of the profession of teacher in China. Han Yu's main argument was that no one will be born with full knowledge, and therefore everyone would need an instructor who "transmitted the Way", "handed down the cause (of Confucian thought)" and solved questions. As a transmitter of the Way, a teacher was required to be himself of the possession of the Confucian Way, not only in theory, but also in practice. He had to refrain from discerning between rich and poor, nobles and commoners, and had to practice the Confucian virtues of benevolence and righteousness.

Also, it is absurd that a person would choose a teacher for his son out of his love for him, and yet refuse to learn from the teacher himself, thinking it a disgrace to do so. The teacher of his son teaches the child only reading and punctuation, which is not propagating the doctrine or resolving doubts as the aforementioned. Han Yu did't think it wise to learn from the teacher when one doesn't know how to punctuate, but not when one has doubts unresolved, for that he found to be the folly of learning in small matters, but neglecting the big ones. He believed that "anyone who was born after me and learned the doctrine before me is also my teacher. Since what I desire to learn is the doctrine, why should I care whether he was born before or after me? Therefore, it does not matter whether a person is high or low in position, young or old in age. Where there is the doctrine, there is my teacher", as the ancient sages did not limit themselves to particular teachers: Confucius had learned from people who were not as virtuous and talented as him.

A student had to seek advice from different teachers, to balance their opinions, had to empty his heart to be open for everything, and not to be ashamed to ask people of lower standing. In this context, Han Yu stressed the ancient principle already established by Confucius, that there had to be a mutual learning between teacher and students, so that both parts progressed towards the finding of the truth, and both sides profited from each other.

---

① The Chinese character "师" has a lot of meaning with varies in different context even within this article its self. It can mean teacher(n.), learning/making a person my teacher(v.) etc.

READING

师　说

韩　愈

　　古之学者①必有师。师者，所以传道②受业解惑也。人非生而知之者，孰能无惑？惑而不从师，其为惑也，终不解矣。生乎吾前，其闻道也固先乎吾，吾从而师之；生乎吾后，其闻道也亦先乎吾，吾从而师之。吾师道③也，夫庸知其年之先后生于吾乎？是故无贵无贱，无长无少，道之所存，师之所存也。

　　嗟乎！师道之不传也久矣，欲人之无惑也难矣。古之圣人，其出人也远矣，犹且从师而问焉；今之众人，其下圣人也亦远矣，而耻学于师。是故圣益圣，愚益愚。圣人之所以为圣，愚人之所以为愚，其皆出于此乎？爱其子，择师而教之；于其身也，则耻师焉，惑矣。彼童子之师，授之书而习其句读者，非吾所谓传其道解其惑者也。句读之不知，惑之不解，或师焉，或不焉，小学而大遗，吾未见其明也。巫医④乐师百工之人，不耻相师。士大夫之族，曰师曰弟子云者，则群聚而笑之。问之，则曰："彼与彼年相若也，道相似也，位卑则足羞，官盛则近谀。"呜呼！师道之不复，可知矣。巫医乐师百工之人，君子不齿，今其智乃反不能及，其可怪也欤！

　　圣人⑤无常师。孔子师郯子⑥、苌弘⑦、师襄⑧、老聃⑨。郯子之徒，其贤不及孔子。孔子曰：三人行，则必有我师。是故弟子不必不如师，师不必贤于弟子。闻道有先后，术业有专攻，如是而已。

　　李氏子蟠，年十七，好古文，六艺⑩经传皆通习之，不拘于时，学于余。余嘉其能行古道，作《师说》以贻之。

---

①Here the connotation of "学者" should not be confused with that in modern Chinese language, namely "scholar" or "student"; as in ancient Chinese language, it simply means "someone who wants to learn" (may not necessarily learning in academic world, under a proper schooling system or institution).

②Propagate the doctrine of Confucian teachings.

③"师道": the tradition of learning from the teacher, the "道" here carries the meaning of tradition or trend instead of "way" or "path".

④"巫医": witch doctors, they are those who use witchcrafts or black magic to cure illnesses, ask blessings and perform rituals during religious occasions in ancient times.

⑤"圣人": ancient sages, the morally well-educated, virtuous wise men in the tradition of Confucianism, normally referring to the sagely kings Yao (尧), Shun (舜), Yu of Xia Dynasty (夏禹), Tang of Shang Dynasty (商汤), King Wen (文王), King Wu (武王), Duke Zhou (周公) from Zhou Dynasty, Confucius (孔子), etc.

⑥"郯子": Tanzi, the king of the State of Tan during the Spring and Autumn Period.

⑦"苌弘": Changhong, an official during the reign of Emperor Jing of the Zhou Dynasty. Confucius learned from him about music.

⑧"师襄": Shixiang, an official of music in the State of Lu, Confucius learned from him how to play qin.

⑨"老聃": Laodan, another name of Laotse. Confucius learned from him about the rites.

⑩"六艺": six classical works of Confucian teachings.

Session Two *Emile*

Jean-Jacques Rousseau

ABOUT THE AUTHOR

Jean-Jacques Rousseau remains an important figure in the history of philosophy, both because of his contributions to political philosophy and moral psychology and because of his influence on later thinkers. Rousseau's own view of philosophy and philosophers was firmly negative, seeing philosophers as the post-hoc rationalizers① of self-interest, as apologists for various forms of tyranny, and as playing a role in the alienation of the modern individual from humanity's natural impulse to compassion. The concern that dominates Rousseau's work is to find a way of preserving human freedom in a world where human beings are increasingly dependent on one another for the satisfaction of their needs. This concern has two dimensions: material and psychological, of which the latter has greater importance. In the modern world, human beings come to derive their very sense of self from the opinion of others, a fact which Rousseau sees as corrosive of freedom and destructive of individual authenticity.

His *Discourse on Inequality* and *The Social Contract* are cornerstones in modern political and social thought. Rousseau's sentimental novel *Julie*, or *The New Heloise* (1761) was important to the development of pre-romanticism② and romanticism in fiction. Rousseau's autobiographical writings—the posthumously published *Confessions* (composed in 1769), which initiated the modern autobiography, and the unfinished *Reveries of the Solitary Walker* (composed 1776–1778)—exemplified the late-18th-century "Age of Sensibility", and featured an increased focus on subjectivity③ and introspection that later characterized modern writing.

In his mature work, he principally explores two routes to achieving and protecting freedom: the first is a political one aimed at constructing political institutions that allow for the co-existence of free and equal citizens in a community where they themselves are sovereign; the second is a project for child development and education that fosters autonomy

---

①Rationalize (redirected from rationalizers): to explain rationally, e.g., "Philosophy is essentially the endeavor of the human mind to rationalize the universe. (Francis E. Abbot)

②Romanticism: an artistic and intellectual movement originating in Europe in the late 1700s and characterized by a heightened interest in nature, emphasis on the individual's expression of emotion and imagination, departure from the attitudes and forms of classicism, and rebellion against established social rules and conventions.

③Subjectivity: judgment based on individual personal impressions and feelings and opinions rather than external facts, e.g., "The sensation of pain is a highly subjective experience that varies by culture as well as by individual temperament and situation. (John Hoberman)"

and avoids the development of the most destructive forms of self-interest. However, though Rousseau believes the co-existence of human beings in relations of equality and freedom is possible, he is consistently and overwhelmingly pessimistic that humanity will escape from a dystopia of alienation, oppression, and unfreedom. In addition to his contributions to philosophy, Rousseau was active as a composer and a music theorist, as the pioneer of modern autobiography, as a novelist, and as a botanist. Rousseau's appreciation of the wonders of nature and his stress on the importance of feeling and emotion made him an important influence on and anticipator of the romantic movement. To a very large extent, the interests and concerns that mark his philosophical work also inform these other activities, and Rousseau's contributions in ostensibly non-philosophical fields often serve to illuminate his philosophical commitments and arguments.

ABOUT *EMILE*

Rousseau's ideas about education are mainly expounded in *Emile: or On Education*. In this work, he advances the idea of "negative education", which is a form of "child-centered" education. His essential idea is that education should be carried out, so far as possible, in harmony with the development of the child's natural capacities by a process of apparently autonomous discovery. This is in contrast to a model of education where the teacher is a figure of authority who conveys knowledge and skills according to a pre-determined curriculum. Published in 1762, it launched a revolution in thinking about how society should educate and rear children. Its main tenets—that children must learn in accordance with their developing minds, and that society impedes and corrupts their growth—became rallying cries for educators in France and elsewhere.

Rousseau organized *Emile* into five "Books", each focusing on a different aspect of children's education. As the text unfolds, a fictional student, Emile, appears frequently; his experiences make vivid Rousseau's approach to education. Emile outlines principles of child development that resonate with today's research. His argument that young men ought to grow up to be self-reliant and compassionate, instead of manipulative and greedy, offered a ready-made template for the type of good citizens sought by the burgeoning liberty movement of his era.

READING

Book Ⅰ - Birth to Age 5 (Excerpts)

God makes all things good; man meddles with them and they become evil[①]. He forces one soil to yield the products of another, one tree to bear another's fruit. He confuses and confounds time, place, and natural conditions. He mutilates his dog, his horse, and his

---

①Meddles with: to interfere with someone or something; to mess around with someone or something.

slave. He destroys and defaces all things; he loves all that is deformed and monstrous; he will have nothing as nature made it①, not even man himself, who must learn his paces like a saddle-horse, and be shaped to his master's taste like the trees in his garden. Yet things would be worse without this education, and mankind cannot be made by halves. Under existing conditions a man left to himself from birth would be more of a monster than the rest. Prejudice, authority, necessity, example, all the social conditions into which we are plunged, would stifle nature in him and put nothing in her place. She would be like a sapling chance sown in the midst of the highway, bent hither and thither and soon crushed by the passers-by.

Tender, anxious mother② I appeal to you. You can remove this young tree from the highway and shield it from the crushing force of social conventions③. Tend and water it ere④ it dies. One day its fruit will reward your care. From the outset raise a wall round your child's soul; another may sketch the plan, you alone should carry it into execution.

Plants are fashioned⑤ by cultivation, man by education. If a man were born tall and strong, his size and strength would be of no good to him till he had learnt to use them; they would even harm him by preventing others from coming to his aid;⑥ left to himself he would

---

①Words like "force", "confuse", "confound", "mutilate", "destroy" are used by the author to illustrate his point that man meddles with things and have nothing as nature made it.

②The earliest education is most important and it undoubtedly is woman's work. If the author of *Nature* had meant to assign it to men he would have given them milk to feed the child. Address your treatises on education to the women, for not only are they able to watch over it more closely than men, not only is their influence always predominant in education, its success concerns them more nearly, for most widows are at the mercy of their children, who show them very plainly whether their education was good or bad. The laws, always more concerned about property than about people, since their object is not virtue but peace, the laws give too little authority to the mother. Yet her position is more certain than that of the father, her duties are more trying; the right ordering of the family depends more upon her, and she is usually fonder of her children. There are occasions when a son may be excused for lack of respect for his father, but if a child could be so unnatural as to fail in respect for the mother who bore him and nursed him at her breast, who for so many years devoted herself to his care, such a monstrous wretch should be smothered at once as unworthy to live. You say mothers spoil their children, and no doubt that is wrong, but it is worse to deprave them as you do. The mother wants her child to be happy now. She is right, and if her method is wrong, she must be taught to be better. Ambition, avarice, tyranny, the mistaken foresight of fathers, their neglect, their harshness, are a hundredfold more harmful to the child than the blind affection of the mother. Moreover, I must explain what I mean by a mother and that explanation follows.

③Social convention: a set of agreed, stipulated or generally accepted social norms, norms, standards or criteria, often taking the form of a custom. Certain types of rules or customs may become law, and regulatory legislation may be introduced to formalize or enforce the convention.

④Ere: (old use or literary) before.

⑤Fashion: to give shape or form to.

⑥Like them in externals, but without speech and without the ideas which are expressed by speech, he would be unable to make his wants known, while there would be nothing in his appearance to suggest that he needed their help.

die of want before he knew his needs. We lament the helplessness of infancy; we fail to perceive that the race would have perished had not man begun by being a child.

We are born weak, we need strength; helpless, we need aid; foolish, we need reason. All that we lack at birth, all that we need when we come to man's estate, is the gift of education.

This education comes to us from nature, from men, or from things. The inner growth of our organs and faculties is the education of nature, the use we learn to make of this growth is the education of men, what we gain by our experience of our surroundings is the education of things.

Thus we are each taught by three masters. If their teaching conflicts, the scholar is ill-educated and will never be at peace with himself; if their teaching agrees, he goes straight to his goal, he lives at peace with himself, he is well-educated.

Now of these three factors in education nature is wholly beyond our control, things are only partly in our power; the education of men is the only one controlled by us; and even here our power is largely illusory, for who can hope to direct every word and deed of all with whom the child has to do.

Book Ⅲ - Age 12 to Age 15 (Excerpts)

Human intelligence is finite, and not only can no man know everything, he cannot even acquire all the scanty① knowledge of others. Since the contrary of every false proposition is a truth, there are as many truths as falsehoods.② We must, therefore, choose what to teach as well as when to teach it. Some of the information within our reach is false, some is useless, some merely serves to puff up its possessor. The small store which really contributes to our welfare alone deserves the study of a wise man, and therefore of a child whom one would have wise. He must know not merely what is, but what is useful.

From this small stock we must also deduct those truths which require a full grown mind for their understanding, those which suppose a knowledge of man's relations to his fellow-men—a knowledge which no child can acquire; these things, although in themselves true, lead an inexperienced mind into mistakes with regard to other matters.

We are now confined to a circle, small indeed compared with the whole of human thought, but this circle is still a vast sphere when measured by the child's mind. Dark places of the human understanding, what rash hand shall dare to raise your veil?③ What pitfalls④ does our so-called science prepare for the miserable child. Would you guide him along this dangerous path and draw the veil from the face of nature? Stay your hand. First make sure that neither he nor you will become dizzy. Be ware of the specious charms of error and the

---

①Scanty: small or insufficient in amount, size, or extent.

②This sentence means that like false propositions, the number of truths is endless as well.

③Here it means that the reasoning of human being is limited, which leads to the incompleteness of understanding the world.

④Pitfall: an unapparent source of trouble or danger; a hidden hazard.

intoxicating① fumes of pride. Keep this truth ever before you—Ignorance never did any one any harm, error alone is fatal, and we do not lose our way through ignorance but through self-confidence.

His progress in geometry② may serve as a test and a true measure of the growth of his intelligence, but as soon as he can distinguish between what is useful and what is useless, much skill and discretion are required to lead him towards theoretical studies. For example, would you have him find a mean proportional③ between two lines, contrive that he should require to find a square equal to a given rectangle; if two mean proportionals are required, you must first contrive to interest him in the doubling of the cube. See how we are gradually approaching the moral ideas which distinguish between good and evil. Hitherto④ we have known no law but necessity, now we are considering what is useful; we shall soon come to what is fitting and right.

Let us transform our sensations into ideas, but do not let us jump all at once from the objects of sense to objects of thought. The latter are attained by means of the former. Let the senses be the only guide for the first workings of reason. No book but the world, no teaching but that of fact. The child who reads ceases to think, he only reads. He is acquiring words not knowledge.

Teach your scholar⑤ to observe the phenomena of nature; you will soon rouse his curiosity, but if you would have it grow, do not be in too great a hurry to satisfy this curiosity. Put the problems before him and let him solve them himself. Let him know nothing because you have told him, but because he has learnt it for himself. Let him not be taught science, let him discover it. If ever you substitute authority for reason he will cease to reason; he will be a mere plaything of other people's thoughts.

You wish to teach this child geography and you provide him with globes, spheres, and maps⑥. What elaborate preparations! What is the use of all these symbols; why not begin by showing him the real thing so that he may at least know what you are talking about?

One fine evening we are walking in a suitable place where the wide horizon gives us a full view of the setting sun, and we note the objects which mark the place where it sets. Next morning we return to the same place for a breath of fresh air before sun-rise. We see the rays of light which announce the sun's approach; the glow increases, the east seems

---

①Intoxicate: to impair the physical and mental faculties of (a person) by means of alcohol or a drug or other chemical substance.

②Geometry: the mathematics of the properties, measurement, and relationships of points, lines, angles, surfaces, and solids.

③Proportional: Geometric Mean, especially: the square root (such as x) of the product of two numbers (such as a and b) when expressed as the means of a proportion (such as $a/x = x/b$).

④Hitherto: up to this time; until now.

⑤Scholar: student, a person who attends a school or studies under a teacher.

⑥Globes, spheres, and maps: geography teaching aids.

afire, and long before the sun appears the light leads us to expect its return. Every moment you expect to see it. There it is at last! A shining point appears like a flash of lightning and soon fills the whole space; the veil of darkness rolls away, man perceives his dwelling place in fresh beauty. During the night the grass has assumed a fresher green; in the light of early dawn, and gilded by the first rays of the sun, it seems covered with a shining network of dew reflecting the light and colour. The birds raise their chorus of praise to greet the Father of life, not one of them is mute; their gentle warbling① is softer than by day, it expresses the languor② of a peaceful waking. All these produce an impression of freshness which seems to reach the very soul. It is a brief hour of enchantment which no man can resist; a sight so grand, so fair, so delicious, that none can behold it unmoved.

Never tell the child what he cannot understand: no descriptions, no eloquence, no figures of speech, no poetry. The time has not come for feeling or taste. Continue to be clear and cold; the time will come only too soon when you must adopt another tone.

Brought up in the spirit of our maxims③, accustomed to make his own tools and not to appeal to others until he has tried and failed, he will examine everything he sees carefully and in silence. He thinks rather than questions. Be content, therefore, to show him things at a fit season; then, when you see that his curiosity is thoroughly aroused, put some brief question which will set him trying to discover the answer.

On the present occasion when you and he have carefully observed the rising sun, when you have called his attention to the mountains and other objects visible from the same spot, after he has chattered freely about them, keep quiet for a few minutes as if lost in thought and then say, "I think the sun set over there last night; it rose here this morning. How can that be? " Say no more; if he asks questions, do not answer them; talk of something else. Let him alone, and be sure he will think about it.

Remember that this is the essential point in my method—Do not teach the child many things, but never to let him form inaccurate or confused ideas. I care not if he knows nothing provided he is not mistaken, and I only acquaint him with truths to guard him against the errors he might put in their place. Reason and judgment come slowly, prejudices flock to us in crowds, and from these he must be protected. But if you make science itself your object, you embark on an unfathomable④ and shoreless ocean, an ocean strewn with reefs from which you will never return. When I see a man in love with knowledge, yielding to its charms and flitting from one branch to another unable to stay his steps, he seems to me like a child gathering shells on the sea-shore, now picking them up, then throwing them aside for others which he sees beyond them, then taking them again, till overwhelmed by their

---

①Warble: a melodious succession of low pleasing sounds, a musical trill.
②Languor: it mental or physical tiredness or lack of activity.
③Maxim: refers to general truth, fundamental principle, or rule of conduct.
④Unfathomable: difficult or impossible to understand; incomprehensible.

number and unable to choose between them, he flings them all away and returns empty handed.

I have said already that purely theoretical science is hardly suitable for children, even for children approaching adolescence; but without going far into theoretical physics, take care that all their experiments are connected together by some chain of reasoning, so that they may follow an orderly sequence in the mind, and may be recalled at need; for it is very difficult to remember isolated facts or arguments, when there is no cue for their recall.

In your inquiry into the laws of nature always begin with the commonest and most conspicuous phenomena, and train your scholar not to accept these phenomena as causes but as facts. I take a stone and pretend to place it in the air; I open my hand, the stone falls. I see Emile watching my action and I say, "Why does this stone fall?"

What child will hesitate over this question? None, not even Emile, unless I have taken great pains to teach him not to answer. Everyone will say, "The stone falls because it is heavy." "And what do you mean by heavy?" "That which falls." "So the stone falls because it falls?" Here is a poser for my little philosopher①. This is his first lesson in systematic physics, and whether he learns physics or no it is a good lesson in common-sense.

Book Ⅳ - Age 15 to Age 20 (Excerpts)

Self-love is always good, always in accordance with the order of nature. The preservation of our own life is specially entrusted to each one of us, and our first care is, and must be, to watch over our own life; and how can we continually watch over it, if we do not take the greatest interest in it?

Self-preservation requires, therefore, that we shall love ourselves; we must love ourselves above everything, and it follows directly from this that we love what contributes to our preservation. Every child becomes fond of its nurse; Romulus② must have loved the she-wolf who suckled him. At first this attachment is quite unconscious; the individual is attracted to that which contributes to his welfare and repelled by that which is harmful; this is merely blind instinct.③ What transforms this instinct into feeling, the liking into love, the aversion into hatred, is the evident intention of helping or hurting us. We do not become passionately attached to objects without feeling, which only follow the direction given them; but those from which we expect benefit or injury from their internal disposition, from their will, those we see acting freely for or against us, inspire us with like feelings to those they exhibit towards us.

---

①Philosophy has always played an essential role in the development of physics. It was from theoretical mathematics, accurate astronomy and sophisticated philosophy that sprang ancient physics, an attempt to explain the world and uncover the laws that governed the universe.

②In Roman mythology, Romulus and Remus, twin sons of the princess and vestal Rhea Silvia and the god Mars, are the legendary founders of Rome. After their birth, the boys were found by a she-wolf called Lupa who nursed them in her lair in Palatine Hill until they were found by a shepherd and his wife, who raised them as shepherds.

③It means that going after gain/profit and avoiding harm is human nature.

Something does us good, we seek after it; but we love the person who does us good; something harms us and we shrink from it, but we hate the person who tries to hurt us.

The child's first sentiment is self-love, his second, which is derived from it, is love of those about him; for in his present state of weakness he is only aware of people through the help and attention received from them. At first his affection for his nurse and his governess is mere habit. He seeks them because he needs them and because he is happy when they are there; it is rather perception than kindly feeling. It takes a long time to discover not merely that they are useful to him, but that they desire to be useful to him, and then it is that he begins to love them.

I can only find one satisfactory way of preserving the child's innocence, to surround him by those who respect and love him. Without this all our efforts to keep him in ignorance fail sooner or later; a smile, a wink, a careless gesture tells him all we sought to hide; it is enough to teach him to perceive that there is something we want to hide from him. The delicate phrases and expressions employed by persons of politeness assume a knowledge which children ought not to possess, and they are quite out of place with them, but when we truly respect the child's innocence we easily find in talking to him the simple phrases which befit him.

So pity① is born, the first relative sentiment which touches the human heart according to the order of nature. To become sensitive and pitiful the child must know that he has fellow-creatures who suffer as he has suffered, who feel the pains he has felt, and others which he can form some idea of, being capable of feeling them himself. Indeed, how can we let ourselves be stirred by pity unless we go beyond ourselves, and identify ourselves with the suffering animal, by leaving, so to speak, our own nature and taking his. We only suffer so far as we suppose he suffers; the suffering is not ours but his. So no one becomes sensitive till his imagination is aroused and begins to carry him outside himself.

What should we do to stimulate and nourish this growing sensibility, to direct it, and to follow its natural bent? Should we not present to the young man objects on which the expansive force of his heart may take effect, objects which dilate it, which extend it to other creatures, which take him outside himself? Should we not carefully remove everything that narrows, concentrates, and strengthens the power of the human self? That is to say, in other words, we should arouse in him kindness, goodness, pity, and beneficence, all the gentle and attractive passions which are naturally pleasing to man; those passions prevent the growth of envy, covetousness, hatred, all the repulsive and cruel passions which make our sensibility not merely a cipher② but a minus quantity, passions which are the curse of those who feel them.

---

①Pity: it means sympathetic sorrow for one suffering, distressed, or unhappy instead of something to be regretted.

②cipher: one that has no weight, worth, or influence.

I think I can sum up the whole of the preceding reflections in two or three maxims, definite, straightforward, and easy to understand.

FIRST MAXIM.—It is not in human nature to put ourselves in the place of those who are happier than ourselves, but only in the place of those who can claim our pity.

SECOND MAXIM.—We never pity another's woes① unless we know we may suffer in like manner ourselves.

THIRD MAXIM.—The pity we feel for others is proportionate②, not to the amount of the evil, but to the feelings we attribute to the sufferers.

COMPREHENSION & EXERCISES

Ⅰ. **Read "On the Teacher" and try to explain the following terms in English.**

师道

传道

授业

解惑

不耻下问

教学相长

Ⅱ. **Read *Emile* and judge whether the following statements are true or false.**

1. According to Rousseau, one of the most important works of parents for the children from birth to Age 5 is to protect them from the crushing force of social conventions.

2. Rousseau assumes that the children's education comes to us from nature, from men, or from society.

3. Rousseau describes the beauty of sun-rise in order to show the greatness of nature with admiration.

4. Rousseau believes theoretical science is ideally suited for children.

5. According to Rousseau, our first care in life is self-love and to watch over our own life.

Ⅲ. **Translate the following paragraph(in *Emile*) which describes the beauty of sun-rise.**

Next morning we return to the same place for a breath of fresh air before sun-rise. We see the rays of light which announce the sun's approach; the glow increases, the east seems afire, and long before the sun appears the light leads us to expect its return. Every moment you expect to see it. There it is at last! A shining point appears like a flash of lightning and soon fills the whole space; the veil of darkness rolls away, man perceives his dwelling place in fresh beauty. During the night the grass has assumed a fresher green; in the light of early dawn, and gilded by the first rays of the sun, it seems covered with a shining network of dew reflecting the light and colour. The birds raise their chorus of praise to greet the Father of life, not one of them is mute; their gentle warbling is softer than by day, it expresses the

---

① woe: grief, regret, or distress.

② proportionate: being in due proportion.

languor of a peaceful waking. All these produce an impression of freshness which seems to reach the very soul. It is a brief hour of enchantment which no man can resist; a sight so grand, so fair, so delicious, that none can behold it unmoved.

Ⅳ. **Discuss the following questions.**

1. It seems that the roles of teacher in HanYu and Rousseau's works are a little bit different. Tell the differences and explain the possible reasons.

2. "Everyone will say, 'The stone falls because it is heavy.' 'And what do you mean by heavy?' 'That which falls.' 'So the stone falls because it falls?' Here is a poser for my little philosopher." This is a typical Socratic method in teaching. What it is and how can a teacher use it in the classroom?

3. Traditional early childhood education in China currently faces both internal and external challenges changing family structures and increased influence of foreign ideas and values. Parents often want their children to begin academic work and theoretical study early, believing it will give these a head start in the competitive struggle for scholastic success-considered the major route to future opportunities. Is this helpful or harmful? Think about it from a Rousseau's viewpoint.

4. According to Rousseau, experience is more important than reason in the education of children. Do you agree? Why or why not?

5. To stimulate and nourish innate growing sensibility, Rousseau gives three MAXIMS of pity. Do you think these ideas are still feasible and worthy in today's society? Why or why not?

6. Compare and contrast the "love" in *Emile* (Book Ⅳ in particular) with the "benevolence" in Confucianism. For your reference, here are more quotations from Confucian classics:

子路入,子曰:"由,知者若何?仁者若何?"子路对曰:"知者使人知己,仁者使人爱己。"子曰:"可谓士矣。"子贡入,子曰:"赐,知者若何?仁者若何?"子贡对曰:"知者知人,仁者爱人。"子曰:"可谓士君子矣。"颜渊入,子曰:"回,知者若何?仁者若何?"颜渊对曰:"知者自知,仁者自爱。"子曰:"可谓明君子矣。"

——《荀子·子道》

君子务本,本立而道生。孝弟也者,其为仁之本与。

——《论语·学而》

君子以仁存心,以礼存心。仁者爱人,有礼者敬人。爱人者,人恒爱之,敬人者,人恒敬之。

——《孟子·离娄下》

亲亲而仁民,仁民而爱物。

——《孟子·尽心上》

Session Three (Extensive Reading)　　On Education[①]

Albert Einstein

　　A day of celebration generally is in the first place dedicated to retrospect, especially to the memory of personages who have gained special distinction for the development of the cultural life. This friendly service for our predecessors must indeed not be neglected, particularly as such a memory of the best of the past is proper to simulate the well-disposed of today to a courage's effort. But this should be done by someone who, from his youth, has been connected with this State and is familiar with its past, not by one who like a gypsy has wondered about and gathered his experiences in all kinds of countries.

　　Thus there is nothing else left for me but to speak about such questions as, independently of space and time, always have been and will be connected with educational matters. In this attempt I cannot lay any claim to being an authority, especially as intelligent and well-meaning men of all times have dealt with educational problems and have certainly repeatedly expressed their view clearly about these matters. From what source shall I, as a partial layman in the realm of pedagogy, derive courage to expound opinions with no foundations except personal experience and personal conviction? If it were really a scientific matter, one would probably be tempted to silence by such considerations.

　　However, with the affairs of active human beings it is different. Here knowledge of truth alone does not suffice; on the contrary this knowledge must continually be renewed by ceaseless effort, if it is not be lost. It resembles a statue of marble which stands in the desert and is continually threatened with burial by the shifting sand. The hands of service must ever be at work, in order that the marble continues lastingly to shine in the sun. To these serving hands mine shall also belong.

　　The school has always been the most important means of transferring the wealth of tradition from one generation to the next. This applies today in an even higher degree than in former time, for through modern development of the economic life, the family as bearer of tradition and education has been weakened. The continuance and health of human society is therefore in a still higher degree dependent on the school than formerly.

　　Sometimes one sees in the school simply the instrument for transferring a certain maximum quantity of knowledge to the growing generation. But that's not right. Knowledge is dead; the school, however, serves the living. It should develop in the young individuals

---

　　[①]Excerpts from an address by Albert Einstein to the State University of New York at Albany, on the occasion of the celebration of the tercentenary of higher education in America, 15th October, 1931. "Ideas and Opinions" by Albert Einstein.

those equalities and capabilities which are of value for the welfare of the commonwealth. But that does not mean that individuality should be destroyed and the individual becomes a mere tool of the community, like a bee or an ant. For a community of standardized individuals without personal originality and personal aims would be a poor community without possibilities for development. On the contrary, the aim must be the training of independently thinking and acting individuals, who, however, see in the service of the community their highest life problem.

But how shall one try to attain this ideal? Should one perhaps try to realize this aim by moralizing? Not at all. Words are and remain empty sound, and the road to perdition has ever been accompanied by lip service to an ideal. But personalities are not formed by what is heard and said but by labor and activity.

The most important method of education accordingly always has consisted of the where pupil was urged to actual performance. This applies as well to the first attempts at writings of the primary boy as to the doctor's thesis on graduation from the university, or as to the mere memorizing of a poem, the writing of a composition, the interpretation and translation of a text, the solving of a mathematical problem or the practice of a physical sport.

But behind every achievement exists the motivation which is at the foundation of it and, which in turn is strengthened and nourished by the accomplishment of the undertaking. Here, there are the greatest differences and they are of greatest importance to the education value of the school. The same work may owe its origin to fear and compulsion, ambitious desire for authority and distinction, or loving interest in the object and a desire for truth and understanding, and thus to that divine curiosity which every healthy child possesses, but which so often is weakened early. The educational influence which is exercised upon the pupil by the accomplishment of one and the same work may be widely different, depending upon whether fear of hurting egoistic passion, or desire for pleasure and satisfaction is at the bottom of this work. And nobody will maintain that the administration of the school and the attitude of the teachers do not have an influence upon the molding of the psychological foundation for pupils.

To me the worst thing seems to be for a school principally to work with methods of fear, force, and artificial authority. Such treatment destroys the sound sentiments, the sincerity, and the self-confidence of the pupil. It produces the submissive subject. It is not so hard to keep the school free from the worst of all evils. Give into the power of the teacher the fewest possible coercive measures, so that the only source of the pupil's respect for the teacher is the human and intellectual qualities of the latter.

The second-named motive, ambition or, in milder terms, the aiming at recognition and consideration, lies firmly fixed in human nature. With absence of mental stimulus of this kind, human cooperation would be entirely impossible; the desire for approval of one's fellow-man certainly is one of the most important binding powers of society. In this complex of feelings, constructive and destructive forces lie closely together. Desire for approval and recognition is a healthy motive but the desire to be acknowledged as better, stronger, or more intelligent than a fellow being or fellow scholar easily leads to an excessively egoistic psychological adjustment, which may become injurious for the individual and for the community. Therefore the school and the teacher must guard against employing the easy method of creating individual ambition, in order to induce the pupils to diligent work.

Darwin's theory of the struggle for existence and the selectivity connected with it has by many people been cited as authorization of the encouragement of the spirit of competition. Some people also in such a way have tried to prove pseudo-scientifically the necessity of the destructive economic struggle of competition between individuals. But this is wrong, because man owes his strength in the struggle for existence to the fact that he is a socially living animal. As little as a battle between single ants of an ant hill is essential for survival, just so little is this the case with the individual members of a human community.

Therefore, one should guard against preaching to the young man success in the customary sense as the aim of life. For a successful man is he who receives a great deal from his fellow men, usually incomparably more than corresponds to his service to them. The value of a man, however, should be seen in what he gives and not what he is able to receive.

The most important motive for work in the school and in life is pleasure in work, pleasure in its results, and the knowledge of the value of the result to the community. In the awakening and strengthening of the psychological forces in the young man, I see the most important task given by the school. Such a psychological foundation alone leads to a joyous desire for the highest possessions of men, knowledge and artist-like workmanship.

The awakening of the productive psychological powers is certainly less easy than the practice of force or the awakening of individual ambition but is the more valuable for it. The point is to develop the childlike inclination for play and the childlike desire for recognition and to guide the child over to the important fields for society; it is that education which in the main is founded upon the desire for successful activity and acknowledgement. If the school succeeds in working successfully from such points of view, it will be highly honored by the rising generation and the tasks given by the school will be submitted to as a sort of gift. I have known children who preferred schooltime to vacation.

Such a school demands from the teacher that he be a kind of artist in his province. What can be done that this spirit be gained in the school? For this there is just as little a universal remedy as there is for an individual to remain well. But there are certain necessary conditions which can be met. First, teachers should grow up in such schools. Second, the teacher should be given extensive liberty in the selection of the material to be taught and the methods of teaching employed by him. For it is true also of him that pleasure in the shaping of his work is killed by force and exterior pressure.

If you have followed my meditations up to this point, you will probably wonder about one thing. I have spoken fully about what spirit, according to my opinion, youth should have instructed. But I have said nothing yet about the choice of subjects for instruction, nor about the method of teaching. Should language predominate or the technical education in science?

To this I answer: in my opinion all this is of secondary importance. If a young man has trained his muscles and physical endurance by gymnastics and walking, he will later be fitted for every physical work. This is also analogous to the training of the mind and of the mental and manual skill. Thus, the wit was not wrong who defined education in this way: "Education is that which remains, if one has forgotten everything he learned in school." For this reason I am not at all anxious to take sides in the struggle between the followers of the classical philologic-historical education and the education more devoted to natural science.

On the other hand, I want to oppose the idea that the school has to teach directly that special knowledge and those accomplishments which one has to use later directly in life. The demands of life are much too manifold to let such a specialized training in school appear possible. Apart from that, it seems to me, moreover, objectionable to treat the individual like a dead tool. The school should always have as its aim that the young man leave it as a harmonious personality, not as a specialist. This in my opinion is true in a certain sense even for technical schools, whose students will devote themselves to a quite definite profession. The development of general ability for independent thinking and judgement should always be placed foremost, not the acquisition of special knowledge. If a person masters the fundamentals of his subject and has learned to think and work independently, he will surely find his way and besides will better be able to adapt himself to progress and changes than the person whose training principally consists in the acquiring the detailed knowledge.

Finally, I wish to emphasize once more that what has been said here in a somewhat categorical form does not claim to mean more than the personal opinion of a man, which is founded upon nothing but his own personal experience, which he has gathered as a student and as a teacher.

Unit Five   Poetry

诗者,志之所之也,在心为志,发言为诗,情动于中而形于言,言之不足,故嗟叹之,嗟叹之不足,故咏歌之,咏歌之不足,不知手之舞之,足之蹈之也。

——《毛诗序》

The poem is that to which what is intently on the mind goes. In the mind it is "being intent"; coming out in language, it is a poem. The affections are stirred within and take on form in words. If words alone are inadequate, we speak them out in sighs. If sighing is inadequate, we sing them. If singing them is inadequate, unconsciously our hands dance them and our feet tapthem.

—"The Great Preface" to *The Book of Songs*

Poetry is the spontaneous overflow of powerful feelings: it takes its origin from emotion recollected in tranquillity: the emotion is contemplated till by a species of reaction, the tranquillity gradually disappears, and an emotion, kindred to that which was before the subject of contemplation, is gradually produced, and does itself actually exist in the mind.

—William Wordsworth (English Romantic poet)

Session One
"The Great Preface" to *The Book of Songs* (Mao Shi Xu)

ABOUT *THE BOOK OF SONGS*

The Book of Songs (also called *The Book of Poetry*) is a compilation of popular and aristocratic songs dating from the early Zhou period. It contains 305 poems that are classified as popular songs, ballads① (feng, "wind"), court odes② (ya, "elegant"), or hymns③ (song). The popular songs are said to have been collected on the orders of the early Zhou kings as a way of gauging the feelings of their subjects. Thus, even the songs that are thought to have their roots in folk song and poetry are likely to have been modified by a scholarly official and may not be in their original form. Nonetheless, the songs give us a rich and varied view of the lives and concerns of commoners and of the elite of the Zhou dynasty. The compilation had taken on roughly the form that we see today by 544 B.C.

The ballads (Feng) are shorter lyrics in simple language that are generally ancient folk songs which record the voice of the common people. They often speak of love and courtship, longing for an absent lover, soldiers on campaign, farming and housework, and political satire and protest. On the other hand, court odes (Ya) and hymns (Song) tend to be longer ritual or sacrificial songs, usually in the forms of courtly panegyrics④ and dynastic odes which praise the founders of the Zhou dynasty. They also include odes used in sacrificial rites and songs used by the aristocracy in their sacrificial ceremonies or at banquets.

Court odes contains "Lesser Odes⑤" and "Greater Odes⑥". Most of the poems were used by the aristocracies to pray for good harvests each year, worship gods, and venerate their ancestors. The author of "Major Courtly Songs" are nobilities who were dissatisfied with the political reality. Therefore, they wrote poems not only related to the feast, worship, and epic but also to reflect the public feelings.

ABOUT "THE GREAT PREFACE"

"The Great Preface"⑦ to *The Book of Songs*, was the most authoritative statement on the nature and function of poetry in traditional China. Not only was it to be the beginning of every student's study of *The Book of Songs* from the Eastern Han through the Sung, its

---

①风。
②雅。
③颂。
④a public speech or published text in praise of someone or something.
⑤小雅。
⑥大雅。
⑦大序。

concerns and terminology became an essential part of writing about poetry and learning about poetry. It was one text on the nature of poetry that everyone knew from the end of the Han on; and even when "the Great Preface" came under harsh attack in later ages, many positions in it remained almost universally accepted.

In *The Book of Songs*, a short "Lesser Preface", ① preceding each poem announces its provenance② and original purpose; and "the Great Preface" as we now have it, has been integrated into or replaces the "Lesser Preface" to the first poem. It is uncertain exactly when "the Great Preface" reached its present form, but we can be reasonably sure that it was no later than the first century A.D. Many readers accepted "the Great Preface" as the work of Confucius' disciple Zixia③ and thus saw in it an unbroken tradition of teaching about the Book of Songs that could be traced back to Confucius himself. A more learned and skeptical tradition took "the Great Preface" as the work of one Wei Hung, a scholar of the first century A.D. It is probably anachronistic④ to apply the concept of "composition" (except in its root sense of "putting together" to "the Great Preface", rather, "the Great Preface" is a loose synthesis of shared "truths" about *The Book of Songs*, truths which were the common possession of traditionalists (whom we now call "Confucians") in the Warring States and the Western Han periods. In their oral transmission these truths were continually being reformulated; the moment when they were written down as "the Great Preface" may be considered that stage in their transmission when reformulation changed into exegesis⑤.

READING

《毛诗序》

《关雎》,后妃之德⑥也,风之始也,所以风天下而正夫妇也。故用之乡人焉,用之邦国焉。风⑦,风也,教也,风以动之,教以化之。

诗者,志之所之也,在心为志,发言为诗,情动于中而形于言,言之不足,故嗟叹之,嗟叹之

---

①小序。

②the history of ownership of a work of art or literature.

③Bu Shang (507B.C. – 400B.C.), commonly known by his courtesy name Zixia, was an ancient Chinese philosopher and a prominent disciple of Confucius who was considered one of the most accomplished in cultural learning. He was one of the five disciples who took chief responsibility for the transmission of Confucius' teachings. He played a significant role in the transmission of such classics as *the Book of Poetry* and *the Book of Change*.

④chronologically misplaced.

⑤critical explanation or interpretation of a text, especially of scripture.

⑥"后妃之德": the virtue of the Queen Consort.

⑦"风": airs, which are shorter lyrics in simple language that are generally ancient folk songs which record the voice of the common people.

不足,故咏歌之,咏歌之不足,不知手之舞之足之蹈之也。

情发于声,声成文谓之音,治世之音安以乐,其政和①;乱世之音怨以怒,其政乖②;亡国之音哀以思,其民困③。故正得失,动天地,感鬼神,莫近于诗。先王以是经夫妇,成孝敬,厚人伦,美教化,移风俗。

故诗有六义④焉:一曰风,二曰赋,三曰比,四曰兴,五曰雅,六曰颂。上以风化下,下以风刺上,主文而谲谏,言之者无罪,闻之者足以戒,故曰风。至于王道衰⑤,礼义废⑥,政教失⑦,国异政⑧,家殊俗⑨,而变风变雅作矣。国史⑩明乎得失之迹,伤人伦之废,哀刑政之苛⑪,吟咏情性,以风其上⑫,达于事变而怀其旧俗也。故变风发乎情,止乎礼义。发乎情,民之性也;止乎礼义,先王之泽也。是以一国之事,系一人之本,谓之风;言天下之事,形四方之风,谓之雅⑬。雅者,正也,言王政之所由废兴也。政有大小,故有小雅焉,有大雅焉。颂者,美盛德之形容,以其成功告于神明者也。是谓四始,诗之至也。

SELECTIONS FROM THE BOOK OF SONGS

郑风·将仲子

将仲子兮,无逾我里⑭,无折我树杞。岂敢爱⑮之?畏⑯我父母。仲可怀也,父母之言,亦可畏也。

将仲子兮,无逾我墙,无折我树桑。岂敢爱之?畏我诸兄。仲可怀也,诸兄之言,亦可畏也。

---

①"治世之音安以乐,其政和": the tones of a well-managed age are at rest and happy; its government is balanced.

②"乱世之音怨以怒,其政乖": the tones of an age of turmoil are bitter and full of anger; its government is perverse.

③"亡国之音哀以思,其民困": the tones of a ruined state are filled with lament and brooding; its people are in difficulty.

④"六义": six principles in the poems, which are airs (feng); exposition(fu); comparison(bi); affective Image(xing); Odes(ya); Hymns(song).

⑤"王道衰": when the royal way declined.

⑥"礼义废": rites and moral principles were abandoned.

⑦"政教失": policies of benevolence were declined; etiquette and education abandoned.

⑧"国异政": each vassal state went its oun way without coordination.

⑨"家殊俗": the customs of each vassal state were different.

⑩"国史": the historians of the states.

⑪"伤人伦之废,哀刑政之苛": they were pained by the abandonment of proper human relations and lamented the severity of punishments and governance.

⑫"吟咏情性,以风其上": they sang their feelings to criticize those above.

⑬"言天下之事,形四方之风,谓之雅": to speak of the affairs of the whole world and to describe customs (feng) common to all places is called Ya. Ya means "proper".

⑭"无逾我里": Do not climb into our homestead.

⑮"爱": to cherish something.

⑯"畏": to be afraid of something.

将仲子兮,无逾我园,无折我树檀。岂敢爱之?畏人之多言。仲可怀也,人之多言,亦可畏也。①

魏风·硕鼠

硕鼠硕鼠,无食我黍②!三岁贯女③,莫我肯顾④。逝将去女⑤,适彼乐土。乐土乐土,爰得我所⑥。

硕鼠硕鼠,无食我麦!三岁贯女,莫我肯德⑦。逝将去女,适彼乐国。乐国乐国,爰得我直⑧?

硕鼠硕鼠,无食我苗!三岁贯女,莫我肯劳⑨。逝将去女,适彼乐郊。乐郊乐郊,谁之永号⑩?

秦风·蒹葭

蒹葭苍苍,白露为霜。所谓伊人,在水一方。溯洄从之,道阻且长⑪。溯游从之,宛在水中央⑫。

蒹葭萋萋,白露未晞。所谓伊人,在水之湄。溯洄从之,道阻且跻⑬。溯游从之,宛在水中坻⑭。

蒹葭采采,白露未已。所谓伊人,在水之涘。溯洄从之,道阻且右⑮。溯游从之,宛在水中沚⑯。

---

① "仲可怀也,人之多言,亦可畏也":Chung Tzu I dearly love;But of all that people will say, indeed I am afraid.
② "黍":millet.
③ "三岁贯女":three years we have slaved for you.
④ "莫我肯顾":yet you take no notice of us.
⑤ "逝将去女":at last we are going to leave you.
⑥ "爰得我所":we shall have our place.
⑦ "莫我肯德":yet you give us no credit.
⑧ "爰得我直":where we shall get our due.
⑨ "莫我肯劳":yet you did nothing to reward us.
⑩ "乐郊乐郊,谁之永号":happy borders, happy borders; where no sad songs are sung.
⑪ "溯洄从之,道阻且长":I went up the river to look for him, but the way was difficult and long.
⑫ "溯游从之,宛在水中央":I went down the stream to look for him, and there in mid-water, sure enough, it's he!
⑬ "溯洄从之,道阻且跻":Up stream I sought him; but the way was difficult and steep.
⑭ "溯游从之,宛在水中坻":Down stream I sought him, and away in mid-water, there on a ledge, that's he!
⑮ "溯洄从之,道阻且右":Up stream I followed him, but the way was hard and long.
⑯ "溯游从之,宛在水中沚":Down stream I sought him, and away in mid-water, there on the shoals is he!

Session Two Preface to Lyrical Ballads

William Wordsworth

ABOUT THE AUTHOR

William Wordsworth (1770A.D.-1850A.D.) was an English Romantic poet who, with Samuel Taylor Coleridge, helped to launch the Romantic Age in English literature with their joint publication *Lyrical Ballads* (1798).

William Wordsworth was born on 7 April 1770 at Cockermouth in Cumbria. His father was a lawyer. Both Wordsworth's parents died before he was 15, and he and his four siblings were left in the care of different relatives. As a young man, Wordsworth developed a love of nature, a theme reflected in many of his poems.

While studying at Cambridge University, Wordsworth spent a summer holiday on a walking tour in Switzerland and France. He became an enthusiast for the ideals of the French Revolution. He began to write poetry while he was at school, but none was published until 1793.

In 1795, Wordsworth received a legacy from a close relative and he and his sister Dorothy went to live in Dorset. Two years later they moved again, this time to Somerset, to live near the poet Samuel Taylor Coleridge, who was an admirer of Wordsworth's work. They collaborated on *Lyrical Ballads*, published in 1798. This collection of poems, mostly by Wordsworth but with Coleridge contributing "The Rime of the Ancient Mariner", is generally taken to mark the beginning of the Romantic movement in English poetry.

In 1799, after a visit to Germany with Coleridge, Wordsworth and Dorothy settled at Dove Cottage in Grasmere in the Lake District. Coleridge lived nearby with his family. Wordsworth's most famous poem, "I Wandered Lonely as a Cloud" was written at Dove Cottage in 1804.

In 1802, Wordsworth married a childhood friend, Mary Hutchinson. The next few years were personally difficult for Wordsworth. Two of his children died, his brother was drowned at sea and Dorothy suffered a mental breakdown. His political views underwent a transformation around the turn of the century, and he became increasingly conservative, disillusioned by events in France culminating in Napoleon Bonaparte taking power.

In 1813, Wordsworth moved from Grasmere to nearby Ambelside. He continued to write poetry, but it was never as great as his early works. After 1835, he wrote little more. In 1842, he was given a government pension and the following year became poet laureate. Wordsworth died on 23 April 1850 and was buried in Grasmere churchyard. His great autobiographical poem, "The Prelude", which he had worked on since 1798, was published after his death.

ABOUT THE "PREFACE TO LYRICAL BALLADS"

"Preface to Lyrical Ballads" is an essay by William Wordsworth. In 1798 Wordsworth wrote, with Samuel Taylor Coleridge, the poetry collection *Lyrical Ballads*. Believing that the poems were so novel in theme and style that they required some explanation, Wordsworth wrote a prefatory essay to accompany the second edition of the poems in 1800; he then expanded the essay for the third edition of 1802.

The "Preface" is often considered a manifesto of the Romantic movement in English literature. Wordsworth explains his intention in his poems to express incidents from everyday life in everyday language and imbued with poetic sentiment. He defines poetry as a "spontaneous overflow of powerful feelings" and the poet as "a man speaking to men". Because poetry speaks of universal human emotions, it should usediction that is natural rather than artificial and self-consciously literary. Thus, Wordsworth sets himself apart from classicist poets who addressed an elite audience in language that was tied to formal rules. Wordsworth argues that poetry and prose should be close in style and that the aim of poetry should be to imitate nature and inspire emotion in the reader in a way that emphasizes pleasure. In the final part of the essay, Wordsworth outlines the procedure whereby a poet may observe the world around them and compose poetry through deep reflection on their experiences.

READING

The principal object, then, proposed in these Poems was to choose incidents and situations from common life, and to relate or describe them, throughout, as far as was possible in a selection of language really used by men, and, at the same time, to throw over them a certain colouring of imagination, whereby ordinary things should be presented to the mind in an unusual aspect; and, further, and above all, to make these incidents and situations interesting by tracing in them, truly though not ostentatiously, the primary laws of our nature: chiefly, as far as regards the manner in which we associate ideas in a state of excitement. Humble and rustic life was generally chosen, because, in that condition, the essential passions of the heart find a better soil in which they can attain their maturity, are less under restraint, and speak a plainer and more emphatic language; because in that condition of life our elementary feelings coexist in a state of greater simplicity, and, consequently, may be more accurately contemplated, and more forcibly communicated; because the manners of rural life germinate from those elementary feelings, and, from the necessary character of rural occupations, are more easily comprehended, and are more durable; and, lastly, because in that condition the passions of men are incorporated with the beautiful and permanent forms of nature. The language, too, of these men has been adopted (purified indeed from what appear to be its real defects, from all lasting and rational causes of dislike or disgust) because such men hourly communicate with the best objects from which the best part of language is originally derived; and because, from their rank in society and the sameness and narrow circle of their intercourse, being less under the influence of social vanity, they convey their feelings and notions in simple and unelaborated expressions. Accordingly, such a language, rising out of repeated experience and regular feelings, is a more permanent, and a far more philosophical language, than that which is frequently substituted for it by Poets, who think that they are conferring honour upon themselves and their art, in proportion as they separate themselves from the sympathies of men, and indulge in arbitrary and capricious habits of expression, in order to furnish food for fickle tastes, and fickle appetites, of their own creation.

    I cannot, however, be insensible to the present outcry against the triviality and meanness, both of thought and language, which some of my contemporaries have occasionally introduced into their metrical① compositions; and I acknowledge that this defect, where it exists, is more dishonourable to the writer's own character than false refinement or arbitrary innovation, though I should contend at the same time, that it is far less pernicious② in the sum of its consequences. From such verses the Poems in these volumes will be found distinguished at least by one mark of difference, that each of them has a worthy purpose. Not that I always began to write with a distinct purpose formerly conceived; but habits of meditation have, I trust, so prompted and regulated my feelings, that my descriptions of such objects as strongly excite those feelings, will be found to carry along with them a *purpose*. If this opinion be erroneous, I can have little right to the name of a Poet. For all good poetry is the spontaneous overflow of powerful feelings: and though this be true, Poems to which any value can be attached were never produced on any variety of subjects but by a man who, being possessed of more than usual organic sensibility, had also thought long and deeply. For our continued influxes of feeling are modified and directed by our thoughts, which are indeed the representatives of all our past feelings; and, as by contemplating the relation of these general representatives to each other, we discover what is really important to men, so, by the repetition and continuance of this act, our feelings will be connected with important subjects, till at length, if we be originally possessed of much sensibility, such habits of mind will be produced, that, by obeying blindly and mechanically the impulses of those habits, we shall describe objects, and utter sentiments, of such a nature, and in such connection with each other, that the understanding of the Reader must necessarily be in some degree enlightened, and his affections strengthened and purified.

---

    ①Metrical: of, relating to, or composed in meter.
    ②Pernicious: highly injurious or destructive.

The Solitary Reaper

Behold her, single in the field,
Yon solitary Highland Lass!
Reaping and singing by herself;
Stop here, or gently pass!
Alone she cuts and binds the grain,
And sings a melancholy strain;
O listen! for the Vale profound
Is overflowing with the sound.

No Nightingale did ever chaunt
More welcome notes to weary bands
Of travellers in some shady haunt,
Among Arabian sands:
A voice so thrilling ne'er was heard
In spring-time from the Cuckoo-bird,
Breaking the silence of the seas
Among the farthest Hebrides.

Will no one tell me what she sings? —
Perhaps the plaintive numbers flow
For old, unhappy, far-off things,
And battles long ago:
Or is it some more humble lay,
Familiar matter of to-day?
Some natural sorrow, loss, or pain,
That has been, and may be again?

Whate'er the theme, the Maiden sang
As if her song could have no ending;
I saw her singing at her work,
And o'er the sickle bending;—
I listen'd, motionless and still;
And, as I mounted up the hill,
The music in my heart I bore,
Long after it was heard no more.

My Heart Leaps Up

My heart leaps up when I behold
A rainbow in the sky:
So was it when my life began;
So is it now I am a man;
So be it when I shall grow old,
Or let me die!
The Child is father of the Man;
And I could wish my days to be
Bound each to each by natural piety.

I Wandered Lonely as a Cloud

I wandered lonely as a Cloud
That floats on high o'er Vales and Hills,
When all at once I saw a crowd,
A host of golden Daffodils;
Beside the Lake, beneath the trees,
Fluttering and dancing in the breeze.

Continuous as the stars that shine
And twinkle on the Milky Way,
They stretched in never-ending line
Along the margin of a bay:
Ten thousand saw I at a glance,
Tossing their heads in sprightly dance.

The waves beside them danced, but they
Out-did the sparkling waves in glee:—
A Poet could not but be gay
In such a jocund company:
I gazed—and gazed—but little thought
What wealth the shew to me had brought:

For oft when on my couch I lie

In vacant or in pensive mood,
They flash upon that inward eye
Which is the bliss of solitude,
And then my heart with pleasure fills,
And dances with the Daffodils.

The Sailor's Mother

ONE morning (raw it was and wet—
A foggy day in winter time)
A Woman on the road I met,
Not old, though something past her prime:
Majestic in her person, tall and straight;
And like a Roman matron's was her mien and gait.

The ancient spirit is not dead;
Old times, thought I, are breathing there;
Proud was I that my country bred
Such strength, a dignity so fair:
She begged an alms, like one in poor estate;
I looked at her again, nor did my pride abate.

When from these lofty thoughts I woke,
'What is it,' said I, 'that you bear,
Beneath the covert of your Cloak,
Protected from this cold damp air?'
She anwered, soon as she the question heard,
'A simple burthen, Sir, a little Singing-bird.'

And, thus continuing, she said,
'I had a Son, who many a day
Sailed on the seas, but he is dead';
In Denmark he was cast away:
And I have travelled weary miles to see
If aught which he had owned might still remain for me.

The bird and cage they both were his:

'Twas my Son's bird; and neat and trim
He kept it: many voyages
The singing-bird had gone with him;
When last he sailed, he left the bird behind;
From bodings, as might be, that hung upon his mind.

He to a fellow-lodger's care
Had left it, to be watched and fed,
And pipe its song in safety;—there
I found it when my Son was dead;
And now, God help me for my little wit!
I bear it with me, Sir;—he took so much delight in it.'

COMPREHENSION & EXERCISES

Ⅰ. Read "The Great Preface" to *the Book of Songs* and explain the following terms.

风

雅

颂

大序

小序

六义

Ⅱ. Read the extracts in session two and answer the following questions:

1. According to "the Great Preface", how is poetry created?

2. According to "the Great Preface", how is poetry related to the state of affairs in a country?

3. What can you conclude about the point of view and the identity of the speaker in "Big Rat"?

4. In "Big Rat", what sort of a person is the speaker? What does the speaker do for a living? What is the speaker's social status?

5. What does the "Big Rat" in the poem represent?

6. What is the principal object proposed in *Lyrical Ballads*?

7. Why did Wordsworth choose humble and rustic life as his subject matter?

8. Why did he adopt the language of ordinary men?

9. According to Wordsworth, what is most dishonorable to the writer's own character?

10. In which way did the poems in *Lyrical Ballads* differ from those written by other poets?

11. According to Wordsworth, what is good poetry?

12. What are the similarities and differences in terms of choice of subject matter between *the Book of Songs* and *Lyrical Ballads*?

III. Translate the following paragraph into Chinese.

The principal object, then, proposed in these Poems was to choose incidents and situations from common life, and to relate or describe them, throughout, as far as was possible in a selection of language really used by men, and, at the same time, to throw over them a certain colouring of imagination, whereby ordinary things should be presented to the mind in an unusual aspect; and, further, and above all, to make these incidents and situations interesting by tracing in them, truly though not ostentatiously, the primary laws of our nature: chiefly, as far as regards the manner in which we associate ideas in a state of excitement.

Session Three (Extensive Reading)　Min Shi

明　诗

刘　勰

　　大舜云："诗言志,歌咏言。"圣谟所析,义已明矣。是以"在心为志,发言为诗",舒文载实,其在兹乎?诗者,持也,持人情性。三百之蔽,义归"无邪";持之为训,有符焉尔。

　　人禀七情,应物斯感,感物吟志,莫非自然。昔葛天乐辞,《玄鸟》在曲;黄帝《云门》,理不空弦。至尧有《大唐》之歌,舜造《南风》之诗,观其二文,辞达而已。及大禹成功,九序惟歌;太康败德,五子咸怨:顺美匡恶,其来久矣。自商暨周,雅、颂圆备,四始彪炳,六义环深。子夏监绚素之章,子贡悟琢磨之句,故商赐二子,可与言诗。自王泽殄竭,风人辍采,春秋观志,讽诵旧章,酬酢以为宾荣,吐纳而成身文。逮楚国讽怨,则《离骚》为刺。秦皇灭典,亦造《仙诗》。

　　汉初四言,韦孟首唱,匡谏之义,继轨周人。孝武爱文,柏梁列韵;严、马之徒,属辞无方。至成帝品录,三百余篇,朝章国采,亦云周备。而辞人遗翰,莫见五言,所以李陵、班婕妤,见疑于后代也。按《召南·行露》,始肇半章;孺子《沧浪》,亦有全曲;《暇豫》优歌,远见春秋;《邪径》童谣,近在成世:阅时取证,则五言久矣。又古诗佳丽,或称枚叔,其《孤竹》一篇,则傅毅之词。比采而推,两汉之作也。观其结体散文,直而不野,婉转附物,怊怅切情,实五言之冠冕也。至于张衡《怨篇》,清典可味;《仙诗缓歌》,雅有新声。

　　暨建安之初,五言腾踊,文帝、陈思,纵辔以骋节;王、徐、应、刘,望路而争驱;并怜风月,狎池苑,述恩荣,叙酣宴,慷慨以任气,磊落以使才;造怀指事,不求纤密之巧,驱辞逐貌,唯取昭晰之能。此其所同也。及正始明道,诗杂仙心;何晏之徒,率多浮浅。唯嵇志清峻,阮旨遥深,故能标焉。若乃应璩《百一》,独立不惧,辞谲义贞,亦魏之遗直也。

　　晋世群才,稍入轻绮。张、潘、左、陆,比肩诗衢,采缛于正始,力柔于建安。或析文以为妙,或流靡以自妍,此其大略也。江左篇制,溺乎玄风,嗤笑徇务之志,崇盛忘机之谈,袁孙已下,虽各有雕采,而辞趣一揆,莫与争雄,所以景纯《仙篇》,挺拔而为隽矣。宋初文咏,体有因革。庄老告退,而山水方滋;俪采百字之偶,争价一句之奇,情必极貌以写物,辞必穷力而追新。此近世之所,竞也。

　　故铺观列代,而情变之数可监;撮举同异,而纲领之要可明矣。若夫四言正体,则雅润为本;五言流调,则清丽居宗,华实异用,惟才所安。故平子得其雅,叔夜含其润,茂先凝其清,景阳振其丽,兼善则子建仲宣,偏美则太冲公干。然诗有恒裁,思无定位,随性适分,鲜能通圆。若妙识所难,其易也将至;忽以为易,其难也方来。至于三六杂言,则出自篇什;离合之发,则萌于图谶;回文所兴,则道原为始;联句共韵,则柏梁馀制。巨细或殊,情理同致,总归诗囿,故不繁云。

　　赞曰:

　　民生而志,咏歌所含。兴发皇世,风流二《南》。神理共契,政序相参。英华弥缛,万代永耽。

Unit Six Rhetoric

夫情动而言形,理发而文见,盖沿隐以至显,因内而符外者也。

——刘勰(中国文学理论家、批评家)

When emotion stirs, language takes form. When ideas come, writings appear. Thus the obscure becomes manifest and the internal is externalized.

——Liu Xie(Chinese literary theorist & critic)

The style is the man.

——Georges Buffon(French scientist)

Of the modes of persuasion furnished by the spoken word there are three kinds. The first kind depends on the personal character of the speaker; the second on putting the audience into a certain frame of mind; the third on the proof, provided by the words of the speech itself.

——Aristotle(ancient Greek philosopher and scientist)

Unit Six　Rhetoric

Session One　*Dragon-Carving and Literary Mind*

Liu Xie

ABOUT THE AUTHOR

Liu Xie, courtesy name Yanhe (彦和), was a famous Chinese literary theorist, critic and writer during the Northern and Southern Dynasties. He was the author of China's greatest work of literary aesthetics, *Dragon-Carving and Literary Mind* (文心雕龙).

It is generally assumed that Liu Xie was born between 460 and 480 in Jingkou near Jiankang (present Nanjing) into a distinguished but impoverished family whose members had formerly served in high ranks. The family may have been distantly related to the reigning house of the Han dynasty. Orphaned at an early age, Liu was devoted to learning. He did not marry, but depended on the eminent Buddhist monk Sengyou (僧祐, 445-518) at the Dinglin Temple of Jiankang for more than a decade, assisting him with the cataloging and collation of Buddhist scriptures. After the founding of the Liang dynasty (502), Liu was appointed to various minor offices at court and beyond. The most noteworthy of these positions was interpreter-clerk of the Eastern Palace.

Apart from the *Dragon-Carving and Literary Mind*, only two other texts have survived to this day. One is a stele inscription (a genre in which Liu reportedly excelled), and the other text is a Buddhist apologetic.

ABOUT *DRAGON-CARVING AND LITERARY MIND*

Dragon-Carving and Literary Mind by Liu Xie is the most important early medieval work of literary theory, acclaimed for its deep understanding, elegant diction, and singularly comprehensive approach. It addresses a broad scope of questions, from the lofty workings of the literary imagination down to the depths of typology, illustrated throughout by perceptive, critical references to a vast number of texts through the ages that reveal Liu Xie's outstanding erudition.

Dragon-Carving and Literary Mind is divided into 10 scrolls and 50 chapters. The first five chapters are a kind of general outline of literary theory. All literary writings have to be based on the background of a certain dao/"way" and have to go back to the literary examples of the glorious past. In the following part (chapters 6-chapters 25) Liu Xie describes the development of the various literary styles. The chapters dealing with poetry are of great importance. Yet historiography, masters and treatises are also described in detail. In the subsequent part (chapters 26) the technique of compiling a literary work is dealt with.

The aspect of literary philosophy plays an important part for the position of literary works in the humans world. A successful author has to know about the natural "way" and its spirit. His works integrate a natural innateness of the world order and therefore are an ideal object for study and for education. Such a spirit can be found in the Confucian Classics. The author has to go back to the "way" of nature, take the classics as his prototype, and follow the Saints of antiquity. He advocates a simple and genuine style and suggests that a good author has his own particular style. The evolution of different literary genres, but also the general development of literature follows, as Liu Xie states, the political and social conditions of the time.

For a successful composition it is important to discern between subjective feelings and objective criteria. This was already known in earlier times, but Liu Xie was the first who discussed the art of writing in detail. Literature, in his eyes, had to achieve the same beauty as coloured clouds or blossoming flowers. Adornments are not only an outer appearance but contribute to the naturalness of the work. Any author has to bring with him a natural inclination and talent to write that has to be fostered through practicing and study. The subjective feelings have to be paired with an objective scenery or condition which mutually influence and support each other. Literature is born out of the heart, and it is not possible that feelings are produced for literature. Shape and style of a literary work are accordingly also formed by the emotional intention of the author.

All literary writings can have eight different characters which consists of four pairs of opposites, namely elegant and recondite, concise and plain, ornate and sublime, exotic and frivolous. These pairs of opposites can pass over to each other, so that a work does not necessarily have to stick to one character. Specifically, Modeled on the classics, the elegant style is Confucian, while the recondite with its abstruse diction and ornaments is Daoist. Frugal with words and sentences, the concise style is characterized by precision of analysis; straightforward in language and clear in meaning, the plain style is cogent and to the point. The ornate style is rich in metaphors and resplendent with ornaments; the sublime, expressing lofty ideas in grand designs, dazzles with splendor. The exotic style renounces the old to embrace the new and in so doing treads on strange and dangerous by paths; the frivolous, ostentatious in language but feeble in thought, merely pursues the modish.

In summary, a literary writings has to possess both "spirit" (Feng 风) expressing thoughts and feelings and also a clear, fresh and vigorous structure (Gu 骨). Literary imagination does not have to be too abstract or obscure but has to refer to examples from daily life that every reader might be able to experience or at least to picture himself. The mind of author and reader has to wander slowly but constantly to the envisaged target, it does not have to leave the concrete world and common senses. Finally, Liu summarized that as natural endowments are different, so styles are diverse and uncertain. Language is the skin and flesh, thought the bone and marrow. The elegant and beautiful resemble perfect silk embroideries, the excessive and frivolous are like the mixture of red and purple. Given persistent application, nurture can compensate for nature.

READING

文心雕龙·体性

刘 勰

夫情动而言形,理发而文见,盖沿隐以至显,因内而符外者也。然才有庸俊,气有刚柔,学有浅深,习有雅郑,并情性所烁,陶染所凝,是以笔区云谲,文苑波诡者矣。故辞理庸俊,莫能翻其才;风趣刚柔,宁或改其气;事义浅深,未闻乖其学;体式雅郑,鲜有反其习。各师成心,其异如面。①

若总其归涂,则数穷八体②:一曰典雅,二曰远奥,三曰精约,四曰显附,五曰繁缛,六曰壮丽,七曰新奇,八曰轻靡。典雅者,熔式经诰,方轨儒门者也;远奥者,馥采典文,经理玄宗者也;精约者,核字省句,剖析毫厘者也;显附者,辞直义畅,切理厌心者也;繁缛者,博喻酿采,炜烨枝派者也;壮丽者,高论宏裁,卓烁异采者也;新奇者,摈古竞今,危侧趣诡者也;轻靡者,浮文弱植,缥缈附俗者也。故雅与奇反,奥与显殊,繁与约舛,壮与轻乖,文辞根叶,苑囿其中矣③。

若夫八体屡迁,功以学成。才力居中,肇自血气;气以实志,志以定言,吐纳英华,莫非情性。是以贾生④俊发,故文洁而体清;长卿⑤傲诞,故理侈而辞溢;子云⑥沉寂,故志隐而味深;子政⑦简易,故趣昭而事博;孟坚⑧雅懿,故裁密而思靡;平子⑨淹通,故虑周而藻密;

---

①In this paragraph, Liu believed that when emotion stirs, language takes form, when ideas come, writings appear. Thus the obscure becomes manifest and the internal is externalized. Each writer follows his own heart and the differences between one and another are as clear as different faces: mediocrity or brilliance of language and thought depends on talent, masculinity or effeminacy of style is determined by personality, depth or shallowness of meaning is related to learning, elegance or baseness of style is contingent on cultivation.

②This is the key statement in Liu Xie's stylistic theory.

③An example of Liu Xie's use of organic metaphor in literary discourse.

④Jia Yi (贾谊, 200B.C.-168B.C.), literary scholar and writer of political treatises in the Western Han Dynasty. Here it means that bright and sharp, Jia Yi had a pure and fresh style.

⑤Sima Xiangru (司马相如, 179B.C.-118B.C.), alias rhyme-prose writer of the Western Han Dynasty. Here it means that proud and unrestrained, Sima Xiangru used inflated language to make inflated arguments.

⑥Yang Xiong (扬雄, 53B.C.-18A.D.), alias Ziyun, writer and philosopher in the Western Han Dynasty. Here it means that quiet and pensive, Yang Xiong reached depth beyond his surface meanings.

⑦Liu Xiang (刘向, 77B.C.-6B.C.), alias Zizheng, scholar of Confucian classics and bibliographer in Western Han Dynasty. Here it means that simple and plain, Liu Xiang wrote with clarity and breadth.

⑧Ban Gu (班固, 32A.D.-92A.D.), alias Mengjian, historian and writer in the Eastern Han Dynasty. Here it means that graceful and genial, Ban Gu was good at organization and thorough in thought.

⑨Zhang Heng (张衡, 78A.D.-139A.D.), alias Pingzi, literary scholar and astronomer in the Eastern Han Dynasty. Here it means that learned and erudite, Zhang Heng planned carefully and wrote with precision.

仲宣①躁锐,故颖出而才果;公幹②气褊,故言壮而情骇;嗣宗③倜傥,故响逸而调远;叔夜④俊侠,故兴高而采烈;安仁⑤轻敏,故锋发而韵流;士衡⑥矜重,故情繁而辞隐。触类以推,表里必符,岂非自然之恒资,才气之大略哉!⑦

夫才有天资,学慎始习。斫梓染丝,功在初化;器成彩定,难可翻移。故童子雕琢,必先雅制⑧,沿根讨叶,思转自圆。八体虽殊,会通合数,得其环中,则辐辏相成。故宜摹体以定习,因性以练才。文之司南,用此道也。⑨

赞曰:才性异区,文体繁诡。辞为肤根,志实骨髓⑩。雅丽黼黻,淫巧朱紫。习亦凝真,功沿渐靡。

Session Two *Rhetoric*

Aristotle

ABOUT THE AUTHOR

Aristotle (384B.C. - 322B.C.) ancient Greek philosopher and scientist, one of the greatest intellectual figures of Western history. He was the author of a philosophical and scientific system that became the framework and vehicle for both Christian Scholasticism and medieval Islamic philosophy. Even after the intellectual revolutions of the Renaissance, the Reformation, and

---

①Wang Can (王粲, 177A.D. - 217A.D.), alias Zhongxuan, a literary scholar of late Eastern Han Dynasty. Here it means that restless and pugnacious, Wang Can combined a ready wit with a resolute mind.

②Liu Zhen (刘桢, ? - 217A.D.), alias Gonggan, a literary scholar of late Eastern Han Dynasty. Here it means that narrow-minded by temperament, Liu Zhen was full of emotional intensities and startling language.

③Ruan Ji (阮籍, 210A.D. - 263A.D.), alias Sizong, literary scholar and poet of the state of Wei in the Three Kingdom period. Here it means that free and unfettered, Ruan Ji wrote of the transcendent and the remote.

④Ji Kang (嵇康, 224A.D. - 263A.D.), alias Shuye, literary scholar and musician of the state of Wei in the Three Kingdom period. Here it means that bold and chivalrous, Ji Kang expressed high aspirations in uncompromising terms.

⑤Pan Yue (潘岳, 247A.D. - 300A.D.), alias Anren, literary scholar of the Western Jin Dynasty. Here it means that frivolous yet keen, Pan Yue had a quick wit and ready rhymes.

⑥Lu Ji (陆机, 261A.D. - 303A.D.), alias Shiheng, literary scholar of the Western Jin Dynasty. Here it means that reserved and sedate, Lu Ji couched rich emotions in esoteric words.

⑦It show how a writer's style corresponds to the man, and how his talent and natural endowments affect the style.

⑧Here Liu Xie emphasize the importance of the Confucian classics in literary composition: when a child begins to learn, let him begin with the classics.

⑨In this paragraph, Liu emphasized that although the eight styles differ greatly, they have some common laws which once mastered will function like the hub of a wheel that gathers the spokes. Thus a writer should try different styles to find what suits him best and develop his talent accordingly.

⑩This is another example of organic metaphor.

the Enlightenment, Aristotelian concepts remained embedded in Western thinking.

Aristotle's intellectual range was vast, covering most of the sciences and many of the arts, including biology, botany, chemistry, ethics, history, logic, metaphysics, rhetoric, philosophy of mind, philosophy of science, physics, poetics, political theory, psychology, and zoology. He was the founder of formal logic, devising for it a finished system that for centuries was regarded as the sum of the discipline; and he pioneered the study of zoology, both observational and theoretical, in which some of his work remained unsurpassed until the 19th century. But he is, of course, most outstanding as a philosopher. His writings in ethics and political theory as well as in metaphysics and the philosophy of science continue to be studied, and his work remains a powerful current in contemporary philosophical debate.

A prolific writer, lecturer, and polymath, Aristotle radically transformed most of the topics he investigated. In his lifetime, he wrote dialogues and as many as 200 treatises, of which only 31 survive. These works are in the form of lecture notes and draft manuscripts never intended for general readership. Nevertheless, they are the earliest complete philosophical treatises we still possess.

ABOUT *RHETORIC*

Aristotle's *Rhetoric* is a comprehensive treatise on the art of persuasive speech. It is divided into three books, or sections. Book I establishes the general principles, terminologies, and assumptions that will inform the rest of the work. Aristotle defines "rhetoric", then describes the three main methods of persuasion: logos (logical reasoning), ethos (character), and pathos (emotion). He further subdivides logos into example and enthymeme (a form of syllogism). Aristotle then identifies the three styles of oratory: deliberative (political), forensic (legal), and epideictic (ceremonial). With these basic principles established, the author outlines topics that pertain to each of the three styles of oratory, such as the motives of wrong-doing for forensic oratory.

Book II is the longest in this work, and it provides a detailed investigation of logos, pathos, and ethos. Beginning with pathos, Aristotle focuses on the emotions that could be useful for public speakers, such as anger. The author contends that a thorough understanding of every emotion will help the speaker to excite the desired emotion in his listeners. Regarding ethos, Aristotle describes how age and fortune (as in luck) can affect the characters of men (the speakers and audience are almost always men in the context of ancient Athens). With this knowledge, a speaker can adjust his rhetorical style to appeal most to his target demographic. Furthermore, this understanding allows the speaker to portray his own character in the appropriate way. Ending with logos, the author explores proof through example, concluding that relevant historical events are more useful examples than invented examples, such as fables. Aristotle also argues that example works best as an illustration of enthymeme, rather than as proof in its own right. Enthymeme is Aristotle's preferred form of proof, since it is logically sound and not dependent on external factors beyond the argument itself.

Book Ⅲ in this work deals with lexis (style or delivery) and taxis (arrangement). Regarding style, Aristotle advises the reader to use natural-sounding language and diction that is simple and elegant, and not so overwrought that it sounds poetic. This discussion also involves some aspects of Greek language that do not translate into English. Finally, Aristotle discusses his recommended arrangement for speeches, encompassing a proem (introduction), narrative, argument, and epilogue (conclusion). He explains the best use of the various rhetorical tools within this arrangement, depending on the style of oratory. The work ends abruptly with the conclusion of this discussion.

READING

BOOK III

CHAPTER 2

We have therefore next to speak of style; for it is not sufficient to know what one ought to say, but one must also know how to say it, and this largely contributes to making the speech appear of a certain character. In the first place, following the natural order, we investigated that which first presented itself—what gives things themselves their persuasiveness; in the second place, their arrangement by style; and in the third place, delivery, which is of the greatest importance but has not yet been treated of by anyone. In fact, it only made its appearance late in tragedy and rhapsody①, for at first the poets themselves acted their tragedies.② It is clear, therefore, that there is something of the sort in rhetoric as well as in poetry. Now delivery is a matter of voice, as to the mode in which it should be used for each particular emotion; when it should be loud, when low, when intermediate; and how the tones, that is, shrill, deep, and intermediate, should be used; and what rhythms are adapted to each subject. For there are three qualities that are considered,—volume, harmony③, rhythm. Those who use these properly nearly always carry off the prizes in dramatic contests, and as at the present day actors have greater influence on the stage than the poets. But no treatise has yet been composed on delivery, since the matter of style itself only lately came into notice; and rightly considered it is

---

①Rhapsody: an epic poem adapted for recitation.

②Since the authors of tragedies acted their own plays, there was no need for professional actors, nor for instruction in the art of delivery or acting. This explains why no attempt had been made to deal with the question.

③Harmony: the pleasant combination of different notes of music played at the same time.

thought vulgar①. But since the whole business of Rhetoric is to influence opinion,② we must pay attention to it, not as being right, but necessary; for, as a matter of right, one should aim at nothing more in a speech than how to avoid exciting pain or pleasure. In every system of instruction there is some slight necessity to pay attention to style; for it does make a difference, for the purpose of making a thing clear, to speak in this or that manner.

The poets, as was natural, were the first to give an impulse to style; for words are imitations, and the voice also, which of all our parts is best adapted for imitation, was ready to hand; thus the arts of the rhapsodists, actors, and others, were fashioned.③ And as the poets, although their utterances were devoid of sense, appeared to have gained their reputation through their style, it was a poetical style that first came into being, as that of Gorgias④. Even now the majority of the uneducated think that such persons express themselves most beautifully, whereas this is not the case, for the style of prose is not the same as that of poetry. And the result proves it. It is evident that we need not enter too precisely into all questions of style, but only those which concern such a style as we are discussing. As for the other kind of style⑤, it has already been treated in the Poetics.

In regard to style, one of its chief merits may be defined as perspicuity⑥. This is shown by the fact that the speech, if it does not make the meaning clear, will not perform its proper function; neither must it be mean⑦, nor above the dignity of the subject, but appropriate to it; for the poetic style may be is not mean, but it is not appropriate to prose. Of nouns and verbs it is the proper ones that make style perspicuous⑧; all the others which have been spoken of in the Poetics elevate and make it ornate⑨; for departure from the ordinary makes it appear more dignified. In this respect men feel the same in regard to style as in regard to foreigners and fellow-citizens. Wherefore we should give our language a "foreign air"; for men admire what is remote, and that which excites admiration is pleasant. In poetry many things conduce to this and there it is appropriate; for the subjects and persons spoken of are more out of the common. But in prose such methods are appropriate in much fewer instances, for the subject is less elevated⑩; and even in poetry, if fine language were used by

---

①Vulgar: not having or showing good taste.

②Or, "is concerned with appearance."

③Fashion: make or shape something.

④Greek sophist and rhetorician.

⑤i.e. the poetic style. In Aristotle's Poetics, the choice of words and the extent to which out-of-the-way words and phrases may be used in poetry is discussed.

⑥Perspicuity: clarity, clearness.

⑦Mean: average, not very great.

⑧"Nouns and verbs" is a conventional expression for all the parts of speech.

⑨Ornate: marked by elaborate rhetoric and elaborated with decorative details.

⑩It means that the subject matter of prose, compared with poetry, is usually ordinary, so the flowery language or gorgeous style is not suitable.

a slave or a very young man, or about quite unimportant matters, it would be hardly becoming; for even here due proportion consists in contraction and amplification as the subject requires①. Wherefore② those who practise this artifice③ must conceal it and avoid the appearance of speaking artificially instead of naturally; for that which is natural persuades, but the artificial does not. ④ For men become suspicious of one whom they think to be laying a trap for them, as they are of mixed wines. Art is cleverly concealed when the speaker chooses his words from ordinary language and puts them together like Euripides, who was the first to show the way. ⑤

Nouns and verbs being the components of speech, and nouns being of the different kinds which have been considered in the Poetics, of these we should use strange, compound, or coined words⑥ only rarely and in few places; the reason for this has already been mentioned, namely, that it involves too great a departure from suitable language. Proper and appropriate words and metaphors are alone to be employed in the style of prose; this is shown by the fact that no one employs anything but these. For all use metaphors in conversation, as well as proper and appropriate words; wherefore it is clear that, if a speaker manages well, there will be some thing "foreign" about his speech, while possibly the art may not be detected, and his meaning will be clear. And this, as we have said, is the chief merit of rhetorical language.

CHAPTER 7

Propriety of style will be obtained by the expression of emotion and character, and by proportion to the subject matter. Style is proportionate to the subject matter when neither weighty matters are treated offhand⑦, nor trifling matters with dignity, and no embellishment⑧ is attached to an ordinary word⑨; Style expresses emotion, when a man speaks with anger of wanton⑩ outrage; with indignation⑪ and reserve, even in mentioning

---

①Even in the poetry writing, the style should be changed to fit the subject.

②Wherefore: as a result, for this reason.

③Artifice: clever use of tricks and devices.

④It means that the natural style is persuasive, but affectation is not.

⑤Here it is said that the choice and use of words requires subtlety and care, skill in making an old word new by clever combination being especially praised.

⑥Coined word: A. a new word or phrase or an existing word used in a new sense. B. the introduction or use of new words or new senses of existing words.

⑦Offhand: casually thoughtless or inconsiderate.

⑧Embellishment: the act of adding extraneous decorations.

⑨Appropriate style means not to treat important themes hastily, not to describe unimportant topics too much, and not to polish ordinary words with extraneous decorations.

⑩Wanton: causing harm or damage deliberately.

⑪Indignation: a feeling of anger and surprise.

them, of things foul or impious①; with admiration of things praiseworthy; with lowliness② of things pitiable; and so in all other cases. Appropriate style also makes the fact appear credible; for the mind of the hearer is imposed upon③ under the impression that the speaker is speaking the truth, because, in such circumstances, his feelings are the same, so that he thinks (even if it is not the case as the speaker puts it) that things are as he represents them; and the hearer always sympathizes with one who speaks emotionally, even though he really says nothing. This is why speakers often confound their hearers by mere noise.

Character also may be expressed by the proof from signs, because to each class and habit there is an appropriate style. I mean class in reference to age—child, man, or old man; to sex—man or woman; to country—Lacedaemonian④ or Thessalian⑤. I call habits those moral states which form a man's character in life; for not all habits do this. If then anyone uses the language appropriate to each habit, he will represent the character; for the uneducated man will not say the same things in the same way as the educated.

CHAPTER 14

The object of an appeal to the hearer is to make him well disposed or to arouse his indignation, and sometimes to engage his attention or the opposite; for it is not always expedient⑥ to engage his attention, which is the reason why many speakers try to make their hearers laugh. As for rendering the hearers tractable, everything will lead up to it if a person wishes, including the appearance of respectability, because respectable persons command more attention. Hearers pay most attention to things that are important, that concern their own interests, that are astonishing, that are agreeable; wherefore one should put the idea into their heads that the speech deals with such subjects. To make his hearers inattentive, the speaker must persuade them that the matter is unimportant, that it does not concern them, that it is painful.

CHAPTER 16

And the narrative should be of a moral character, and in fact it will be so, if we know what effects this. One thing is to make clear our moral purpose; for as is the moral purpose, so is the character, and as is the end, so is the moral purpose.⑦ For this reason mathematical treatises have no moral character, because neither have they moral purpose; for they have no moral end. But the Socratic dialogues have; for they discuss such questions. Other ethical indications are the accompanying peculiarities of each individual character. Nor should we

---

①Impious: lacking due respect or dutifulness.

②Lowliness: humbleness.

③Imposed upon: draws a wrong conclusion.

④Lacedaemonian: a native or inhabitant of Lacedaemon, an area of ancient Greece.

⑤Thessalian: a native or inhabitant of the ancient Greek region of Thessaly.

⑥Expedient: useful or necessary.

⑦It means that the narrator's character can be shown through clearly putting forward the moral purpose.

speak as if from the intellect, after the manner of present-day orators; but from moral purpose: "But I wished it, and I preferred it; and even if I profited nothing, it is better." The first statement indicates prudence①, the second virtue; for prudence consists in the pursuit of what is useful, virtue in that of what is honorable.

COMPREHENSION & EXERCISES

Ⅰ. Read *Dragon-Carving and Literary Mind* and try to explain the following eight styles/terms classified by Liu Xie.

典雅

远奥

精约

显附

繁缛

壮丽

新奇

轻靡

Ⅱ. Read the introduction of *Rhetoric* (see "ABOUT RHETORIC") and choose the best answers for the following questions.

1. Which of the following is not one of Aristotle's three rhetorical methods?
   A. Logos   B. Pathos   C. Eros   D. Ethos

2. Rhetoric can easily be found in _____.
   A. Political speeches   B. Advertisements
   C. School essays   D. All of the above

3. The main purpose of rhetoric is _____.
   A. Persuasion   B. Emotional appeal
   C. Inspiration   D. None of the above

4. An argument based purely on emotions would be _____.
   A. Bad rhetoric   B. Logos   C. Pathos   D. All of the above

5. When a piece of literature appeals to your mind and explains things to you logically, it is using its_____.
   A. Ethos   B. Pathos   C. Mind   D. Logos

Ⅲ. Translate the following paragraph (in *Rhetoric*) which describes the property of style.

Propriety of style will be obtained by the expression of emotion and character, and by proportion to the subject matter. Style is proportionate to the subject matter when neither weighty matters are treated offhand, nor trifling matters with dignity, and no embellishment is attached to an ordinary word; Style expresses emotion, when a man speaks with anger of wanton outrage; with indignation and reserve, even in mentioning them, of things foul or

---

① prudence: care and good sense.

impious; with admiration of things praiseworthy; with lowliness of things pitiable; and so in all other cases.

Ⅳ. Discuss the following questions.

1. French scientist Georges Buffon believes that "the style is the man", can you illustrate this idea with the examples given by Liu Xie in *Dragon-Carving and Literary Mind*?

2. Regarding style, in *Rhetoric*, Aristotle advises the reader to use natural-sounding language and diction that is simple and elegant. Do you agree with his suggestion? Why or why not?

3. In *Rhetoric*, Aristotle encourages beautiful-sounding metaphors that are proportional in scope to the object they represent. Can you find the metaphors used by Liu Xie in his *Dragon-Carving and Literary Mind*? To what extent it illustrates that metaphor is an essential tool to lend clarity to Liu's article?

Ⅴ. Writing.

Analyze a famous speech for its use of logos, pathos, and ethos.

Directions: Identify examples in which the speech makes appeals to audience needs and attitudes, and state what behavior or set of actions (if any) the speaker wants the audience to engage in. Estimate the extent to which you could attend fully to this speech without being distracted by the characteristics or qualities of the speaker. Note anything the speaker says that works to enhance the speaker/audience relationship, and state whether it promotes perceptions of the speaker's expertise, trustworthiness, similarity, or attractiveness.

Session Three (Extensive Reading)　*Institutio Oratoria*[①]

Quintilian

　　My aim, then, is the education of the perfect orator. The first essential for such an one is that he should be a good man, and consequently we demand of him not merely the possession of exceptional gifts of speech, but of all the excellences of character as well.

　　For I will not admit that the principles of upright and honourable living should, as some have held, be regarded as the peculiar concern of philosophy. The man who can really play his part as a citizen and is capable of meeting the demands both of public and private business, the man who can guide a state by his counsels, give it a firm basis by his legislation and purge its vices by his decisions as a judge, is assuredly no other than the orator of our quest.

　　Wherefore, although I admit I shall make use of certain of the principles laid down in philosophical textbooks, I would insist that such principles have a just claim to form part of the subject-matter of this work and do actually belong to the art of oratory.

　　I shall frequently be compelled to speak of such virtues as courage, justice, self-control; in fact scarcely a case comes up in which some one of these virtues is not involved; every one of them requires illustration and consequently makes a demand on the imagination and eloquence of the pleader. I ask you then, can there be any doubt that, wherever imaginative power and amplitude of diction are required, the orator has a specially important part to play?

　　These two branches of knowledge were, as Cicero has clearly shown, so closely united, not merely in theory but in practice, that the same men were regarded as uniting the qualifications of orator and philosopher. Subsequently this single branch of study split up into its component parts, and thanks to the indolence of its professors was regarded as consisting of several distinct subjects. As soon as speaking became a means of livelihood and the practice of making an evil use of the blessings of eloquence came into vogue, those who had a reputation for eloquence ceased to study moral philosophy, and ethics, thus abandoned by the orators, became the prey of weaker intellects. As a consequence certain persons, disdaining the toil of learning to speak well, returned to the task of forming character and establishing rules of life and kept to themselves what is, if we must make a division, the

---

　　[①] Quintilian (born 35A.D., Calagurris Nassica, Hispania Tarraconensis—died after 96A.D., Rome) was the celebrated orator and rhetorician from the first century who brought forward rhetorical theory from ancient Greece and from the heyday of Roman rhetoric in the prior century. Quintilian's work on rhetoric, *Institutio Oratoria*, is a major contribution to educational theory and literary criticism.

better part of philosophy, but presumptuously laid claim to the sole possession of the title of philosopher, a distinction which neither the greatest generals nor the most famous statesmen and administrators have ever dared to claim for themselves. For they preferred the performance to the promise of great deeds.

I am ready to admit that many of the old philosophers inculcated the most excellent principles and practised what they preached. But in our own day the name of philosopher has too often been the mask for the worst vices. For their attempt has not been to win the name of philosopher by virtue and the earnest search for wisdom; instead they have sought to disguise the depravity of their characters by the assumption of a stern and austere mien accompanied by the wearing of a garb differing from that of their fellow men.

Now as a matter of fact we all of us frequently handle those themes which philosophy claims for its own. Who, short of being an utter villain, does not speak of justice, equity and virtue? Who (and even common country-folk are no exception) does not make some inquiry into the causes of natural phenomena? As for the special uses and distinctions of words, they should be a subject of study common to all who give any thought to the meaning of language.

But it is surely the orator who will have the greatest mastery of all such departments of knowledge and the greatest power to express it in words. And if ever he had reached perfection, there would be no need to go to the schools of philosophy for the precepts of virtue. As things stand, it is occasionally necessary to have recourse to those authors who have, as I said above, usurped the better part of the art of oratory after its desertion by the orators and to demand back what is ours by right, not with a view to appropriating their discoveries, but to show them that they have appropriated what in truth belonged to others.

Let our ideal orator then be such as to have a genuine title to the name of philosopher: it is not sufficient that he should be blameless in point of character (for I cannot agree with those who hold this opinion): he must also be a thorough master of the science and the art of speaking, to an extent that perhaps no orator has yet attained.

Still we must none the less follow the ideal, as was done by not a few of the ancients, who, though they refused to admit that the perfect sage had yet been found, none the less handed down precepts of wisdom for the use of posterity.

Perfect eloquence is assuredly a reality, which is not beyond the reach of human intellect. Even if we fail to reach it, those whose aspirations are highest, will attain to greater heights than those who abandon themselves to premature despair of ever reaching the goal and halt at the very foot of the ascent.

I have therefore all the juster claim to indulgence, if I refuse to pass by those minor details which are none the less essential to my task. My first book will be concerned with the education preliminary to the duties of the teacher of rhetoric. My second will deal with the rudiments of the schools of rhetoric and with problems connected with the essence of rhetoric itself.

The next five will be concerned with Invention, in which I include Arrangement. The four following will be assigned to Eloquence, under which head I include Memory and Delivery. Finally there will be one book in which our complete orator will be delineated; as far as my feeble powers permit, I shall discuss his character, the rules which should guide him in undertaking, studying and pleading cases, the style of his eloquence, the time at which he should cease to plead cases and the studies to which he should devote himself after such cessation.

In the course of these discussions I shall deal in its proper place with the method of teaching by which students will acquire not merely a knowledge of those things to which the name of art is restricted by certain theorists, and will not only come to understand the laws of rhetoric, but will acquire that which will increase their powers of speech and nourish their eloquence.

For as a rule the result of the dry textbooks on the art of rhetoric is that by straining after excessive subtlety they impair and cripple all the nobler elements of style, exhaust the lifeblood of the imagination and leave but the bare bones, which, while it is right and necessary that they should exist and be bound each to each by their respective ligaments, require a covering of flesh as well.

I shall therefore avoid the precedent set by the majority and shall not restrict myself to this narrow conception of my theme, but shall include in my twelve books a brief demonstration of everything which may seem likely to contribute to the education of an orator. For if I were to attempt to say all that might be said on each subject, the book would never be finished.

There is however one point which I must emphasise before I begin, which is this. Without natural gifts technical rules are useless. Consequently the student who is devoid of talent will derive no more profit from this work than barren soil from a treatise on agriculture.

There are, it is true, other natural aids, such as the possession of a good voice and robust lungs, sound health, powers of endurance and grace, and if these are possessed only to a moderate extent, they may be improved by methodical training. In some cases, however, these gifts are lacking to such an extent that their absence is fatal to all such advantages as talent and study can confer, while, similarly, they are of no profit in themselves unless cultivated by skilful teaching, persistent study and continuous and extensive practice in writing, reading and speaking.

Unit Seven　Love

回眸一笑百媚生，六宫粉黛无颜色。

——白居易（中国唐代诗人）

Turning her head, she smiled so sweet and full of grace.
that she outshone in six palaces the fairest face.

—Bai Juyi(Chinese poet)

At the touch of love everyone becomes a poet.
—Plato(Greek philosopher & founder of the Academy)

For small creatures such as we, the vastness is bearable only through love.
—Karl Sagan (American astronomer & science writer)

Session One *Book of Poetry (Shi Jing)*

ABOUT *BOOK OF POETRY*

*Book of Poetry*① is the earliest existing anthology of poetry in China. It comprises 305 poems dating from the beginning of the Western Zhou period (1046B.C. - 771B.C.) to the mid-Spring and Autumn period (approx. 771B.C. - 476B.C.). This also gives it another name *The Three Hundred Poems*. *Book of Poetry* was deemed as one of the Five Classics of Confucianism in Western Han dynasty (206B.C. - 24 A.D.). The poems mostly originated from areas along the Yellow River, but most of the authors cannot be identified.

Despite various statements (such as royal officials collecting songs or Confucius editing and abridging poems) on the origin of *Book of Poetry*, it is generally acknowledged that *Book of Poetry* are collected by dedicated governmental officers in Zhou Dynasty, then edited and composed with music and dance. Confucius also participated this procedure to a certain extent.

Book of Poetry is composed of three parts: "Feng"(*Book of Poetry*), "Ya"(*Book of Odes and Epics*) and "Song"(*Book of Hyms*). Ya and Song. Feng is the most valued part or essence of *Book of Poetry*, mainly due to its description of the customs, life (such as love and marriage) and other aspects of the society. It includesfolk songs from 15 states, usually with a love theme. Ya is said to be the classical music in the capital area of the Zhou Empire. This part contains 105 poems. "Ya" is divided into "Daya" (Major Odes) and "Xiaoya"(Minor Odes). "Song" consists the songs that the emperor or governors used in events like offering sacrifices to gods or ancestors. It elaborates the achievement of the governing classes, which includes 40 poems in total. The songs collected in *Book of Poetry* are not only of a high literary value as the oldest songs in China, they also reveal much of the activities of different social strata in early China.

While *Book of Poetry*'s music form and genres are "Feng", "Ya", and "Song", its stylistic devices are "Fu", "Bi" and "Xing". Altogether these six terms are also known as "liuyi"(six meanings)②. The great Tang (Dynasty) commentator Kong Yingda③ interprets

---

①*Book of Poetry* has over ten versions of English translation. The most widely known versions are James Legge's *The She King*, published in 1876; Ezra Pound's *Shih-ching*, published in 1915; Arthur Waley's *The Book of Songs*, published in 1937 and Xu Yuanchong's *Book of Poetry*, published in 1993. The annotation in this book is mainly from Xu's version.

②Known in Chinese as "六义", among which, "赋" means "straightforward", a very descriptive and often didactic type of poem; "比" stands for "simile, parable"; "兴" usually comes with an atmospherical introduction.

③孔颖达 in Chinese. He was a Confucian scholar of the early Tang period. He obtained an excellent education from his teacher Liu Zhuo(刘焯) and was well-versed in *the Five Classics* (《五经》).

those terms in the following way: "Feng", "Ya" and "Song" referred to certain external compositional forms or functions, while Fu, Bi and Xing were designations for certain methods of how the content of the poem was approached, or stylistic devices. During the Han period, when only the four designations of "Feng", "Daya", "Xiaoya" and "Song" were used, they were interpreted as the "four beginnings" describing the flourishing and decline of the royal house of Zhou.

Book of Poetry had always attracted the interest of all groups of scholars. Confucius once said that without *Book of Poetry* there was nothing to talk about. It was often cited by him as a model of literary expression, for, despite its numerous themes, the subject matter was always "expressive of pleasure without being licentious, and of grief without being hurtfully excessive"①. It is regarded as "minor words, but in-depth meanings" by Confucianism, however, some modern scholars doubt this over-interpretation of *Book of Poetry*, saying it is not the "bible" of poems, merely a literature masterpiece. The exact meanings of the poems in *Book of Poetry* are very difficult to trace due to the long time passed. What *Book of Poetry* really infers lies on the understanding and interpretation of each reader.

READING

Book of Songs

周 南

关 雎

关关②雎鸠③,在河之洲。
窈窕④淑⑤女,君子好逑⑥。

参差荇菜,左右流⑦之。
窈窕淑女,寤寐⑧求之。

---

①"乐而不淫,哀而不伤" in original text from *The Analects of Confucius* («论语»). It was a comment Confucius gave to "关雎", showing that the sense of happiness and sadness in the poem was not excessive.
②关关:the chirps of both male and female birds.
③雎鸠:turtledoves. Legend has it that the male and the female are inseparable.
④窈窕:(of a woman) gentle and graceful.
⑤淑:(of a woman) fair and with good virtue.
⑥逑:spouse.
⑦流:to follow the water flow to pick it up.
⑧寤寐:being asleep and awake.

求之不得，寤寐思服①。
悠哉悠哉，辗转反侧。

参差荇菜，左右采之。
窈窕淑女，琴瑟友之。

参差荇菜，左右芼②之。
窈窕淑女，钟鼓乐之。

郑 风

狡③童

彼狡童兮，不与我言兮。
维④子之故，使我不能餐兮。

彼狡童兮，不与我食兮。
维子之故，使我不能息兮。

风 雨

风雨凄凄，鸡鸣喈喈。
既见君子，云胡不夷⑤？

风雨潇潇⑥，鸡鸣胶胶。⑧
既见君子，云胡不瘳⑦？

风雨如晦，鸡鸣不已。
既见君子，云胡不喜？

---

①思服：to think about or miss.
②芼：to pick up.
③Handsome yet cunning. there seemed to be an misunderstanding between the poetess and her lover. She adopted this tone to complain about him.
④维：equals "为", meaning "because".
⑤The wind and rain are chill; The crow of cocks is shrill. When I've seen my man best, Should I not feel at rest?
⑥潇潇：to illustrate that the wind is strong and the rain is heavy.
⑦瘳：illness is cured.
⑧Gloomy wind and rain blend; The cocks crow without end. When I have seen my dear, how full I feel of cheer.

子 衿①

青青子衿,悠悠我心。
纵我不往,子宁不嗣②音?

青青子佩,悠悠我思。
纵我不往,子宁不来?

挑兮达兮,在城阙③兮。
一日不见,如三月兮④!

Book of Odes and Epics

鱼藻之什

隰 桑

隰桑有阿⑤,其叶有难。
既见君子,其乐如何!

隰桑有阿,其叶有沃⑥。
既见君子,云何不乐?

隰桑有阿,其叶有幽⑦。
既见君子,德音⑧孔⑨胶⑩。

心乎爱矣,遐不⑪谓矣?
心中藏之,何日忘之?

---

①衿: collar.
②嗣: to send. Here the poet is wondering why her lover is not sending her any word.
③城阙: the city wall.
④I'm pacing up and down on the wall of the town. When to see you I am not free, one day seems like three months to me.
⑤阿: (together with "难" in the next line) supple and graceful.
⑥沃: beautiful and radiant.
⑦幽: dark colored, to show the plant is luxuriant and thriving.
⑧德音: fine words or complimental comments.
⑨孔: very.
⑩胶: (of relationship) solid and close.
⑪遐不: why not.

Session Two *Sonnets*

William Shakespeare

ABOUT THE AUTHOR

William Shakespeare was an English poet and playwright who is considered one of the greatest writers to ever use the English language. He is also the most famous playwright in the world, with his plays being translated in over 50 languages and performed across the globe for audiences of all ages. Known colloquially as "The Bard" or "The Bard of Avon[①]", Shakespeare was also an actor and the creator of the Globe Theatre.

Altogether Shakespeare's works include 38 plays, 2 narrative poems, 154 sonnets, and a variety of other poems. His plays are usually divided into 4 categories: histories, comedies, tragedies, and romances. His earliest plays were primarily comedies and histories such as *Henry VI* and *The Comedy of Errors*. In 1596, Shakespeare wrote *Romeo and Juliet*, his second tragedy, and over the next dozen years he continued writing the plays for which he is now best known: *Julius Caesar, Hamlet, Othello, King Lear, Macbeth*, and *Antony and Cleopatra*. In his final years, Shakespeare turned to the romantic with *Cymbeline, A Winter's Tale*, and *The Tempest*.

Only eighteen of Shakespeare's plays were published separately in quarto editions during his lifetime; a complete collection of his works did not appear until the publication of the First Folio in 1623, several years after his death.

Shakespeare's legacy is as rich and diverse as his work. His plays have spawned countless adaptations across multiple genres and cultures and have had an enduring presence on stage and film. His writings have been compiled in various iterations of The Complete Works of William Shakespeare, which include all of his plays, sonnets, and other poems. William Shakespeare continues to be one of the most important literary figures of the English language.

ABOUT *SHAKESPEARE'S SONNETS*

While Shakespeare was regarded as the foremost dramatist of his time, evidence indicates that both he and his contemporaries looked to poetry, not playwriting, for enduring fame. *Shakespeare's sonnets* were a collection of over 150 works that were published late in his life and without any indication of when each of the pieces was composed. It is widely thought that the sonnets were a part of a private diary that was never meant to be read

---

① A bard is a poet. Avon refers to Shakespeare's birthplace Stratford-upon-Avon.

publicly but nevertheless were published. *Shakespeare's sonnets* were composed between 1593 and 1601, though not published until 1609. That edition, *The Sonnets of Shakespeare*, consists of 154 sonnets, all written in the form of three quatrains and a couplet that is now recognized as Shakespearean①. The possibly autobiographical sonnets are divided into two sections: sonnets 1-126, addressed to a beloved friend, a handsome and noble young man, and sonnets 127-152, to a malignant but fascinating "Dark Lady," who the poet loves in spite of himself. As a narrative, the sonnet sequence tells of strong attachment, of jealousy, of grief at separation, and of joy at being together and sharing beautiful experiences. The Dark Lady sonnets end the sequence on a disturbing note of sorrow and self-loathing. Nearly all of Shakespeare's sonnets examine the inevitable decay of time, and the immortalization of beauty and love in poetry.

Almost all of them love poems, the Sonnets philosophize, celebrate, attack, plead, and express pain, longing, and despair, all in a tone of voice that rarely rises above a reflective murmur, all spoken as if in an inner monologue or dialogue, and all within the tight structure of the English sonnet form.

READING

Sonnets 18

Shall I compare thee to a summer's day?
Thou art more lovely and more temperate②.
Rough winds do shake the darling buds of May,
And summer's lease③ hath all too short a date④.
Sometime too hot the eye of heaven⑤ shines,
And often is his gold complexion dimmed,
And every fair from fair sometime declines⑥,
By chance or nature's changing course untrimmed⑦:

---

① Traditionally, the sonnet is a fourteen-line poem written in iambic pentameter, employing one of several rhyme schemes, and adhering to a tightly structured thematic organization. The name comes from the Italian sonetto, which means "a little sound or song." Two sonnet forms provide the models from which all other sonnets are formed: the Petrarchan and the Shakespearean. The Italian poet Petrarch's sonnet follows the tightly woven rhyme scheme, abba, abba, cdecde or cdcdcd, while the Shakespearean, or English sonnet, follows a different set of rules. Shakespearean sonnets consist of three quatrains and a couplet, following this rhyme scheme: abab, cdcd, efef, gg.

② Temperate: even-tempered, moderate.
③ Lease: temporary period of occupancy.
④ Date: duration.
⑤ Eye of heaven: i.e. the sun.
⑥ Fair: beautiful thing; decline: fade, or lose its beauty.
⑦ Untrimmed: stripped of ornament and beauty.

But thy eternal summer shall not fade
Nor lose possession of that fair thou ow'st①,
Nor shall death brag thou wand'rest in his shade,
When in eternal lines to time thou grow'st②.
So long as men can breathe or eyes can see,
So long lives this③ and this gives life to thee.

Sonnets 33

Full many a glorious morning have I seen
Flatter the mountain-tops with sovereign eye,
Kissing with golden face the meadows green,
Gilding pale streams with heavenly alchemy,
Anon permit the basest clouds to ride④
With ugly rack⑤ on his celestial face,
And from the forlorn world his visage hide,
Stealing unseen to west with this disgrace:
Even so my sun one early morn did shine
With all-triumphant splendour on my brow:
But out, alack⑥, he was but one hour mine,
The region cloud hath masked him from me now.
Yet him for this my love no whit⑦ disdaineth:
Suns of the world may stain when heaven's sun staineth.

Sonnets 73

That time of year thou mayst in me behold
When yellow leaves, or none, or few, do hang
Upon those boughs which shake against the cold,
Bare ruined choirs⑧, where late the sweet birds sang.
In me thou see'st the twilight of such day
As after sunset fadeth in the west,
Which by and by black night doth take away,

---

① Fair thou ow'st: beauty you own.
② To...grow'st: you become an integral part of time.
③ This: this sonnet.
④ Anon: soon; basest: lowliest/darkest.
⑤ Rack: mass of clouds driven by the wind.
⑥ Out, alack: alas.
⑦ No whit: in no way, not at all.
⑧ Choirs: the branches are compared to chancels(choirs), the parts of churches reserved for singers.

Death's second self①, that seals up all in rest②.
In me thou see'st the glowing of such fire
That on the ashes of his youth doth lie,
As the death-bed whereon it must expire,
Consumed with that which it was nourished by.
This thou perceiv'st, which makes thy love more strong,
To love that well which thou must leave ere long③.

Sonnets 130

My mistress' eyes are nothing like the sun;④
Coral is far more red than her lips' red,
If snow be white, why then her breasts are dun⑤,
If hairs be wires, black wires⑥ grow on her head.
I have seen roses damasked⑦, red and white,
But no such roses see I in her cheeks,
And in some perfumes is there more delight
Than in the breath that from my mistress reeks⑧.
I love to hear her speak, yet well I know
That music hath a far more pleasing sound.
I grant I never saw a goddess go:
My mistress when she walks treads on the ground.
And yet, by heaven, I think my love as rare
As any she belied with false compare⑨.

COMPREHENSION & EXERCISES

Ⅰ. Read the above Sonnets and find out the corresponding lines where the following rhetorical devices have been used.

Simile
Metaphor
Hyperbole

---

① Death's second self: i.e. night and sleep.
② Seals…rest: seals people up in sleep as if in a coffin.
③ That: i.e. the poet(and perhaps life/youth); leave: lose/give up.
④ Comparing eyes to the sun is a very common similes in love poetry.
⑤ Dun: grey brown.
⑥ Wires: fine golden wires, used for ornamentation (i.e. in headdresses).
⑦ Damasked: of the damask variety/multicolored(red and white).
⑧ Reeks: exhales(not to imply unpleasant odors at this time).
⑨ She…compare: woman misrepresented by untrue comparisons.

Personification

Puns

Ⅱ. Compare the following two translations of "Sonnet 18" and explain your preference.

阁下比春孰短长？	或许我可用夏日将你作比方，
君更可爱更温良。	但你比夏日更可爱也更温良。
阳春期限叹苦短，	夏风狂作常摧落五月的娇蕊，
娇花五月落风狂。	夏季的期限也未免还不太长。
天眼如炬有时热，	有时天眼如炬人间酷热难当，
金面或暗暂无光。	但转瞬金面如晦，云遮雾障。
人间万美难恒健，	每一种美都终究会凋残零落，
零落随机道无常。	难免见弃于机缘与天道无常。
君有韶华不消褪，	但你永恒的夏季却不会终止，
总葆朱颜独自芳。	你优美的形象也永不会消亡。
阎罗无奈由尔去，	死神难夸口说你深陷其罗网，
尔命永寄在诗行。	只因你借我诗行可长寿无疆。
但有人气人眼亮，	只要人眼能看，人口能呼吸，
君凭我赋万年康。	我诗必长存，使你万世流芳。

——辜正坤《莎士比亚商籁体十四行诗集》

Ⅲ. The exact meanings of the poems in *Book of Poetry* are very difficult to trace due to the long time passed. What it really infers lies on the understanding and interpretation of each reader. Compare the following translations of "Guan Ju" and explain which translation is closer to your own understanding.

1.
Kwan-kwan go the ospreys,
On the islet in the river.
The modest, retiring, virtuous, young lady.
For our prince a good mate she.

Here long, there short, is the duckweed,
To the left, to the right, borne about by the current.
The modest, retiring, virtuous, young lady:
Waking and sleeping, he sought her.

He sought her and found her not,
And walking and sleeping he thought about her.
Long he thought; oh! Long and anxiously;
On his side, on his back, he turned, and back again.

Here long, there short, is the duckweed;

On the left, on the right, we gather it.

The modest, retiring, virtuous, young lady:

With lutes, small and large, let us give her friendly welcome.

Here long, there short, is the duckweed;

On the left, on the right, we cook and present it.

The modest, retiring, virtuous, young lady.

With bells and drums let us show our delight in her.

—*The She King* by James Legge

2.

By riverside a pair

Of turtledoves are cooing;

There is a maiden fair

whom a young man is wooing.

Water flows left and right

Of cresses here and there;

The youth yearns days and night

For the maiden so fair.

His yearning grows so strong,

He cannot fall asleep,

But tosses all night long,

So deep in love, so deep!

Now gather left and right

Cress long or short and tender!

O lute, play music light

For the finance so slender!

Feast friends at left and right

On cresses cooked tender!

O bells and drums, delight

The bride so sweet and slender!

—*Book of Poetry* by Xu Yuanchong

Ⅳ. **Discuss the following questions.**

1. Plant metaphors had been used in Shakespeare's sonnets to express abstract and obscure emotions. *Book of Songs* also contains numerous plant metaphors which were used to vividly describe the poets' emotional world. Find out some examples in the above poems and think about why such similarities are shared by both works.

2. In *Sonnet* 130, instead of playing with poetic conventions in which, for example, the mistress's eyes are compared with the sun, her lips with coral, and her cheeks with roses,

Shakespeare tried to point to another broader point about love within the poem: one should love personality more than looks. Do you think this works better than the traditional way to express one's love? Why or why not?

3. Both *Book of Poetry* and *Shakespeare's sonnets* have been very expressive of the topic of love. Have you noticed any similarities when it comes to expressing one's love?

4. Although *Book of Poetry* has adopted many stylistic devices, "Fu", "Bi" "Xing" are the most well-known techniques. You can refer to the following quotes and explain how these techniques have been employed in the poems in Session One.

赋者,敷也,敷陈其事而直言之者也。比者,以彼物比此物也。兴者,先言他物以引起所咏之词也。

——朱熹《诗集传》

别裁伪体亲风雅,转益多师是汝师。

——杜甫《戏为六绝句》

为诗意如何,六义互铺陈。风雅比兴外,未尝著空文。

——白居易《读张籍古乐府》

大雅久不作,吾衰竟谁陈?

——李白《古风五十九首》

Session Three (Extensive Reading) Of Love[①]

Francis Bacon

The stage is more beholding to love, than the life of man. For as to the stage, love is ever matter of comedies, and now and then of tragedies; but in life it doth much mischief; sometimes like a siren, sometimes like a fury. You may observe that amongst all the great and worthy persons (whereof the memory remaineth, either ancient or recent) there is not one that hath been transported to the mad degree of love; which shows that great spirits and great business do keep out this weak passion. You must except, nevertheless, Marcus Antonius, the half-partner of the empire of Rome, and Appius Claudius, the decemvir and lawgiver; whereof the former was indeed a voluptuous man and inordinate: but the latter was an austere and wise man: and therefore it seems (though rarely) that love can find entrance not only into an open heart, but also into a heart well fortified, if watch be not wellkept. It is a poor saying of Epicurus, Satis magnum aler alteri theatrum sumus; as if man, made for the contemplation of heaven and all noble objects, should do nothing but kneel before a little idol, and make himself subject, though not of the mouth (as beasts are), yet of the eye; which was given him for higher purposes. It is a strange thing to note the excess of this passion, and how it braves the nature and value of things, by this; that the speaking in a perpetual hyperbole is comely in nothing but in love. Neither is it merely in the phrase; for whereas it hath been well said that the arch-flatterer, with whom all the petty flatterers have intelligence, is a man's self certainly the lover is more. For there was never proud man thought so absurdly well of himself as the lover doth of the person loved; and therefore it was well said, That it is impossible to love and to be wise. Neither doth this weakness appear to others only, and not to the party loved, but to the loved most of all, except the love be reciproque. For it is a true rule that love is ever rewarded either with the reciproque or with an inward and secret contempt. By how much the more men ought to beware of this passion, which loseth not only other things, but itself. As for the other losses, the poet's relation doth well figure them: that he that preferred Helena, quitted the gifts of Juno and Pallas. For whosoever esteemeth too much of amorous affection quitteth both riches and wisdom. This passion hath his floods in the very times of weakness; which

---

  ①Excerpt from Francis Bacon's *Essay*, originally published in 1597, and then revised and expanded as *The Essaies of Sr Francis Bacon Knight* in 1612 and as *The Essays or Counsels, Civill and Morall* 1625. The *Essay* covers a variety range of topics, including politics, religions, love, friendship, arts, and education etc. The central theme of this literal work is love and its various effects on those who chase love.

are great prosperity and great adversity (though this latter hath been less observed); both which times kindle love and make it more fervent, and therefore show it to be the child of folly. They do best who, if they cannot but admit love, yet make it keep quarter, and sever it wholly from their serious affairs and actions of life; for if it check once with business, it troubleth men's fortunes, and maketh men that they can no ways be true to their own ends. I know not how, but martial men are given to love: I think it is but as they are given to wine; for perils commonly ask to be paid in pleasures. There is in man's nature a secret inclination and motion towards love of others, which, if it be not spent upon some one or a few, doth naturally spread itself towards many, and maketh men become humane and charitable; as it is seen sometime in friar. Nuptial love maketh mankind; friendly love perfecteth it; but wanton love corrupteth and embaseth it.

Unit Eight   Family

天下之本在国,国之本在家,家之本在身。

——孟子(中国哲学家、思想家)

The root of the world is in the state. The root of the state is in the family. The root of the family is in the person of its head.

—Mengzi (Chinese philosopher)

In family life, love is the oil that eases friction, the cement that binds closer together, and the music that brings harmony.

—Friedrich Nietzsche(German philosopher & cultural critic)

A happy family is but an earlier heaven.

—George Bernard Shaw(Irish playwright & literary critic)

Session One
The Book of Filial Piety (*Xiao Jing*)

ABOUT *THE BOOK OF FILIAL PIETY*

The Book of Filial Piety is one of *Confucian ShiSan Jing* or *the Thirteen Confucian Classics*, and the only one on "filial piety". *The Book of Filial Piety* is one that elaborates on filial piety, laying stress on that "filial piety is the constant law of heaven". Zeng Shen[①], Confucius' disciple, had his definite statement on filial piety: "Of the three ways of filial piety, the greatest is to respect one's parents, the next is not to put one's parents to shame, and the bottommost is to support one's parents financially."[②] Much as *The Book of Filial Piety* maintains that the fundamental virtue of man is to be filial to one's parents, it is to advocate "being loyal" with "filial piety" at the core, including being filial to one's parents at home and being loyal to the sovereign when out.

Scholars' opinions differ on the authorship of the book. It is traditionally attributed to Confucius himself, but this attribution has been doubted since the Southern Song period (1127A. D. - 1279A. D.). It is assumed, instead, that it was compiled by disciples of Confucius or by Confucian scholars at the end of the Warring States (475B. C. - 221B. C.) or in the course of the early Han period (206B. C. - 220B. C.).

The Book of Filial Piety has two versions: *the Old Text*[③] and *the New Text*[④]. The most prevailing copy of the present day is divided into 18 chapters. The central term of the book is filial piety, which is seen as the core concept of the Confucian social system. Nothing was of greater importance than filial piety. With the help of piety, a ruler was able to govern his country justly, and through it all people would bring order and harmony into their families. Filial piety, the relation between father and son, was reflected in the sphere of the state by the relationship between a ruler and his ministers. In this respect, loyalty was the analogue to the principle of filial piety as used in the private sphere. In the relation of two

---

[①] Also known as Zengzi, philosopher, disciple of Confucius, traditionally believed to be the author of the *Daxue* (《大学》). He was highly influential in reaffirming the Confucian emphasis on the virtue of "filial piety" (孝).

[②] "孝有三：大孝尊亲，其次不辱，其下能养" in original text. Here, Zengzi enumerated the three degrees of filial piety: honoring father and mother, not disgracing them, and being able to support them.

[③] *The Old Text* is said to have been discovered in the old house of Confucius. This book was written in the script of the pre-Qin big seal characters, thus gaining the name of *the Old Text*.

[④] *The Book of Filial Piety* was one of the books burned by Qin Shi Huang, the first Emperor of the Qin Dynasty. Luckily, it was preserved and recovered in the Han Dynasty. Some scholars rewrote it in the then prevailing official script and it was known as *the New Text*. In the Western Han Dynasty, Liu Xiang, using *the New Text* as a foundation and with *the Old Text* as a reference, produced a fair copy of the book with more than 1,800 Chinese characters in 18 chapters, which has come down to the present day.

brothers, it could be compared with the love of the younger brother for the elder①.

As a book of traditional Chinese thought of ethics, *The Book of Filial Piety* is the very first one that related filial piety one's parents to loyalty to the sovereign, and stresses that "filial piety" is the foundation of "loyalty", and "loyalty" is the development and elongation of "filial piety". Due to this, this book captured the attention of many emperors.

READING

开宗明义章第一②

仲尼③居,曾子侍。子曰:先王有至德要道,以顺天下,民用和睦,上下无怨。汝知之乎④? 曾子避席曰:参不敏,何足以知之? 子曰:夫孝,德之本也,教之所由生也。复坐,吾语汝。身体发肤,受之父母,不敢毁伤,孝之始也;立身行道,扬名于后世,以显父母,孝之终也;夫孝,始于事亲,中于事君,终于立身。《大雅》⑤云:"无念尔祖,聿修厥德。"⑥

广要道章第十二⑦

子曰:教民亲爱,莫善于孝。教民礼顺,莫善于悌。移风易俗,莫善于乐⑧。安上治民,莫善于礼。礼者,敬而已矣。故敬其父,则子悦;敬其兄,则弟悦;敬其君,则臣悦;敬一人而千万人悦⑨。所敬者寡⑩而悦者众。此之谓要道也。

---

①Here, loyalty means "忠" in Chinese; the love of the younger brother for the elder is called "悌" in Chinese.

②This chapter serves as an introduction and presents the gist or highlight of the book, and all the other following chapters are detailed elaborations or interpretations of this chapter. Filial piety starts with the love for their own physical bodies, as they were given by their parents, and ends with their success in society, which would bring honor and glory to their parents as well as ancestors.

③Confucius.

④The ancient kings applied the greatest virtue and the most important principle to make the common people submit to them. The people lived in harmony, and there were no complaints or grievances between the ruling and the ruled. Do you know how this could be?

⑤"大雅" is one of the part of *Ya (Book of Odes and Epics)* from *Book of Poetry*. The following sentence is from "大雅·文王". This was the first epic ode celebrating King Wen (1184B.C.-1134B.C.), as the founder of the Zhou dynasty. It was attributed to the Duke of Zhou for the benefit of the young King Cheng (1114B.C.-1076B.C.) It showed how King Wen's virtue drew to him the favoring regard of Heaven and made him a bright pattern to his descendants.

⑥Do not forget your ancestors, and cultivate yourself with their virtue.

⑦This chapter is a further elucidation of the most important principle mentioned in the first chapter. This principle includes four aspects: filial piety to parents, respect for elder brothers, music education and the rites.

⑧There is no better way to bring about a change in morals and moves, than to edify and cultivate them into taking up music.

⑨Therefore, respecting others' fathers makes their sons pleased; respecting others' elder brothers makes the younger brothers pleased; respecting others' rulers makes the subjects pleased. Respect for one person will make thousands and thousands of people pleased.

⑩The number is small.

广至德章第十三①

子曰:君子之教以孝也,非家至而日见之也②。教以孝,所以敬天下之为人父者也;教以悌,所以敬天下之为人兄者也;教以臣,所以敬天下之为人君者也。③《诗》云:"恺悌君子,民之父母。"④非至德,其孰能顺民如此其大者乎?

广扬名章第十四⑤

子曰:君子之事亲孝,故忠可移于君;事兄悌,故顺可移于长;居家理,故治可移于官。⑥ 是以行成于内,而名立于后世矣。

Session Two　On Family⑦

Aristotle

ABOUT THE AUTHOR

Aristotle (Greek: Aristoteles), ancient Greek philosopher and scientist, was born in Stagira in northern Greece.

To each of his inquiries he brought the habit of systematic classification, identifying each thing according to its essence—its unique and unchanging nature. He also brought to

---

① This chapter is a further elucidation of the greatest virtue mentioned in the first chapter. The best way of the man of virtue to make people filial to their parents, respectful to their elder brothers and kings is to do it himself.

② "家至" means to go to every house. "日见" means to meet people every day.

③ The aim of him teaching the people to be filial to their parents is to let all the fathers in the world be respected; the aim of him teaching the younger brothers to be respectful to their elder brothers is to let all the elder brothers in the world be respected; the aim of him teaching the subjects to be loyal to their kings is to let all the kings in the world be respected.

④ This sentence is from *Book of Poetry* (大雅·泂酌). This ode was attributed to Duke Kang of Shao for the admonition to King Cheng to fulfill his duties like a parent to his people so that his people may cling to him.

⑤ This chapter further interprets "leaving a good name to posterity", which has been mentioned in the first chapter. Here, Confucius focused on the relationship between being filial and leaving a good name to future generations.

⑥ The man of virtue attends to his parents with filial piety, so he can change his filial piety to his parents into loyalty for the sovereign; he treats his elder brothers with respect, so he can turn his respect for his elder brothers into the reverence for his seniors; at home, he manages his household well, so he can turn his household management into administration of the kingdom.

⑦ Excerpts from Aristotle's *Politics*.

his inquires the exercise of keen observation. He was the founder of formal logic, devising for it a finished system that for centuries was regarded as the sum of the discipline; He gathered specimens of plan and animal life, and classified them according to their physicl similarities. Though he did little in modern scientific experimentation, his practice of basing conclusions on very careful observation advanced the empirical method[1]. He also brought to his analysis of political life, literature and human conduct the same principles he employedin classifying plants and animals: objectivity, clarity and consisency.

ABOUT *POLITICS*

The Politics of Aristotle is the second part of a treatise of which the *Ethics*[2] is the first part. It looks back to the *Ethics* as the *Ethics* looks forward to the *Politics*.

In *Politics*, Aristotle describes the role that politics and the political community must play in bringing about the virtuous life in the citizenry. The aim of the *Politics*, Aristotle says, is to investigate, on the basis of the constitutions collected, what makes for good government and what makes for bad government and to identify the factors favorable or unfavorable to the preservation of a constitution. Aristotle also explained that family was a model for the organization of the state, which made him the first known writer to argue that the natural progression of human beings was from the family via small communities to the polis[3]. In his words, the state is "a community of well-being in families and aggregations of families for the sake of a perfect and self-sufficing life." Thus, the city-state is the natural end of human beings; they start in family groups, progress naturally to forming villages, and finally come together in cities. The family forms the root of human relationships, but the city is the flower.

The *Politics* also provides analysis of the kinds of political community that existed in his time and shows where and how these cities fall short of the ideal community of virtuous citizens.

READING

Book I - Part II

He who thus considers things in their first growth and origin, whether a state or anything

---

[1] Empirical method refers to a method of inquiry dependent on direct experience.

[2] Also known as *Nicomachean Ethics*, in which Aristotle emphasizes the role of habit in conduct. According to him, it is commonly thought that virtues are habits and that the good life is a life of mindless routine.

[3] Polis: literally means "city" in Greek. In Ancient Greece, it originally referred to an administrative and religious city center, as distinct from the rest of the city. Later, it also came to mean the body of citizens under a city's jurisdiction.

else, will obtain the clearest view of them. In the first place there must be a union① of those who cannot exist without each other; namely, of male and female, that the race may continue (and this is a union which is formed, not of deliberate purpose, but because, in common with other animals and with plants, mankind have a natural desire to leave behind them an image of themselves), and of natural ruler and subject, that both may be preserved. For that which can foresee by the exercise of mind is by nature intended to be lord and master, and that which can with its body give effect to such foresight is a subject, and by nature a slave; hence master and slave have the same interest. Now nature has distinguished between the female and the slave. For she is not niggardly, like the smith who fashions the Delphian knife② for many uses; she makes each thing for a single use, and every instrument is best made when intended for one and not for many uses. But among barbarians no distinction is made between women and slaves, because there is no natural ruler among them: they are a community of slaves, male and female. Wherefore the poets say,

"It is meet that Hellenes should rule over barbarians;"③ as if they thought that the barbarian and the slave were by nature one.

Out of these two relationships between man and woman, master and slave, the first thing to arise is the family, and Hesiod④ is right when he says,

"First house and wife and an ox for the plough,"

for the ox is the poor man's slave. The family is the association established by nature for the supply of men's everyday wants, and the members of it are called by Charondas⑤ 'companions of the cupboard,' and by Epimenides⑥ the Cretan, 'companions of the manger.' But when several families are united, and the association aims at something more than the supply of daily needs, the first society to be formed is the village. And the most natural form of the village appears to be that of a colony from the family, composed of the children and grandchildren, who are said to be suckled 'with the same milk.' And this is the reason why Hellenic states were originally governed by kings; because the Hellenes⑦ were under royal rule before they came together, as the barbarians still are. Every family is ruled by the

---

①Union: here it refers to the union of male and female.

②Delphian knife: the meaning to it is uncertain, possibly a dagger and a carving-knife in one.

③Originally from Euripides' *Iphigenia Among the Taurians*. Euripides, Aeschylus and Sophocles are considered to be classical Athens's three great tragic dramatists.

④Hesiod is one of the earliest Greek poets, often called the "father of Greek didactic poetry". The following quote is from one of his existing works: *Works and Days*.

⑤Charondas: lawgiver, a native of Catana. His laws, admired by Aristotle, were used by the cities of Chalcidian foundation in Sicily and Italy.

⑥Epimenides: poet and prophet of Crete, reputed author of religious and poetical writings and other mystical works.

⑦Hellenes: ancient Greek people. Hellenic states refer to the Greek city states in the Classical age, also known as the Hellenic period.

eldest, and therefore in the colonies of the family the kingly form of government prevailed because they were of the same blood. As Homer says:

"Each one gives law to his children and to his wives."①

For they lived dispersedly, as was the manner in ancient times. Wherefore men say that the Gods have a king, because they themselves either are or were in ancient times under the rule of a king. For they imagine, not only the forms of the Gods, but their ways of life to be like their own.

When several villages are united in a single complete community, large enough to be nearly or quite self-sufficing, the state comes into existence, originating in the bare needs of life, and continuing in existence for the sake of a good life. And therefore, if the earlier forms of society are natural, so is the state, for it is the end of them, and the nature of a thing is its end. For what each thing is when fully developed, we call its nature, whether we are speaking of a man, a horse, or a family. Besides, the final cause and end of a thing is the best, and to be self-sufficing is the end and the best.

Hence it is evident that the state is a creation of nature, and that man is by nature a political animal. And he who by nature and not by mere accident is without a state, is either a bad man or above humanity; he is like the

"Tribeless, lawless, hearthless one,"②

whom Homer denounces—the natural outcast is forthwith a lover of war; he may be compared to an isolated piece at draughts③.

Now, that man is more of a political animal than bees or any other gregarious animals is evident. Nature, as we often say, makes nothing in vain, and man is the only animal whom she has endowed with the gift of speech④. And whereas mere voice is but an indication of pleasure or pain, and is therefore found in other animals (for their nature attains to the perception of pleasure and pain and the intimation of them to one another, and no further), the power of speech is intended to set forth the expedient and inexpedient, and therefore likewise the just and the unjust. And it is a characteristic of man that he alone has any sense of good and evil, of just and unjust, and the like, and the association of living beings who have this sense makes a family and a state.

Thus, the state is by nature clearly prior to the family and to the individual, since the whole is of necessity prior to the part; for example, if the whole body be destroyed, there will be no foot or hand, except in an equivocal sense, as we might speak of a stone hand; for

---

①Originally from Homer's *Odessy* (ix. 112-114); also quoted by Plato in his *Laws* (iii 680).

②Originally from *IIliad* (ix. 63). The hearth or the fireplace is seen as a symbol for family by the ancient Greek people. Being an outcast means being abandoned by one's state or village, which is considered to be a very serious penalty.

③Draught: Greek game, very similar to ludus and backgammon.

④Aristotle believed that man, having the gift of speech and the sense of right and wrong, is by nature a political animal.

when destroyed the hand will be no better than that. But things are defined by their working and power; and we ought not to say that they are the same when they no longer have their proper quality, but only that they have the same name. The proof that the state is a creation of nature and prior to the individual is that the individual, when isolated, is not self-sufficing; and therefore he is like a part in relation to the whole. But he who is unable to live in society, or who has no need because he is sufficient for himself, must be either a beast or a god: he is no part of a state. A social instinct is implanted in all men by nature, and yet he who first founded the state was the greatest of benefactors. For man, when perfected, is the best of animals, but, when separated from law and justice, he is the worst of all; since armed injustice is the more dangerous, and he is equipped at birth with arms, meant to be used by intelligence and virtue, which he may use for the worst ends. Wherefore, if he have not virtue, he is the most unholy and the most savage of animals, and the most full of lust and gluttony. But justice is the bond of men in states, for the administration of justice, which is the determination of what is just, is the principle of order in political society.

Book I - Part XII

Of household management we have seen that there are three parts- one is the rule of a master over slaves, which has been discussed already, another of a father, and the third of a husband. A husband and father, we saw, rules over wife and children, both free, but the rule differs, the rule over his children being a royal, over his wife a constitutional rule. For although there may be exceptions to the order of nature, the male is by nature fitter for command than the female, just as the elder and full-grown is superior to the younger and more immature. But in most constitutional states the citizens rule and are ruled by turns, for the idea of a constitutional state implies that the natures of the citizens are equal, and do not differ at all. Nevertheless, when one rules and the other is ruled we endeavor to create a difference of outward forms and names and titles of respect, which may be illustrated by the saying of Amasis about his foot-pan①. The relation of the male to the female is of this kind, but there the inequality is permanent. The rule of a father over his children is royal, for he rules by virtue both of love and of the respect due to age, exercising a kind of royal power. And therefore Homer has appropriately called Zeus 'father of Gods and men,' because he is the king of them all. For a king is the natural superior of his subjects, but he should be of the same kin or kind with them, and such is the relation of elder and younger, of father and son.

Book I - Part XIII(Excerpts)

A similar question may be raised about women and children, whether they too have virtues: ought a woman to be temperate and brave and just, and is a child to be called temperate, and intemperate, or not? So in general we may ask about the natural ruler, and

---

① Amasis king of Egypt was despised by his subjects for his low birth, so he had a statue made out of a gold foot-bath and set it up for them to worship, afterwards explaining to them its lowly origin.

the natural subject, whether they have the same or different virtues. For a noble nature[1] is equally required in both, but if so, why should one of them always rule, and the other always be ruled? Nor can we say that this is a question of degree, for the difference between ruler and subject is a difference of kind, which the difference of more and less never is. Yet how strange is the supposition that the one ought, and that the other ought not, to have virtue! For if the ruler is intemperate and unjust, how can he rule well? If the subject, how can he obey well? If he be licentious and cowardly, he will certainly not do his duty. It is evident, therefore, that both of them must have a share of virtue, but varying as natural subjects also vary among themselves. Here the very constitution of the soul has shown us the way; in it one part naturally rules, and the other is subject, and the virtue of the ruler we in maintain to be different from that of the subject; the one being the virtue of the rational, and the other of the irrational part. Now, it is obvious that the same principle applies generally, and therefore almost all things rule and are ruled according to nature. But the kind of rule differs; the freeman rules over the slave after another manner from that in which the male rules over the female, or the man over the child; although the parts of the soul are present in an of them, they are present in different degrees. For the slave has no deliberative faculty at all; the woman has, but it is without authority, and the child has, but it is immature. So it must necessarily be supposed to be with the moral virtues also; all should partake of them, but only in such manner and degree as is required by each for the fulfillment of his duty. Hence the ruler ought to have moral virtue in perfection, for his function, taken absolutely, demands a master artificer, and rational principle is such an artificer; the subjects, oil the other hand, require only that measure of virtue which is proper to each of them. Clearly, then, moral virtue belongs to all of them; but the temperance of a man and of a woman, or the courage and justice of a man and of a woman, are not, as Socrates maintained the same[2]; the courage of a man is shown in commanding, of a woman in obeying. And this holds of all other virtues, as will be more clearly seen if we look at them in detail, for those who say generally that virtue consists in a good disposition of the soul, or in doing rightly, or the like, only deceive themselves. Far better than such definitions is their mode of speaking, who, like Gorgias[3], enumerate the virtues. All classes must be deemed to have their special attributes; as the poet says of women,

"Silence is a woman's glory,"[4]

---

[1] This word is often used to compliment those of virtues.

[2] Refer to Plato's *Meno* (71B.C. - 73B.C.), which introduces aspects of Socratic ethics and Platonic epistemology in a fictional dialogue that is set among important political events and cultural concerns in the last years of Socrates' life.

[3] *Gorgias* is a Socratic dialogue written by Plato around 380B.C.. The dialogue depicts a conversation between Socrates and a small group of sophists (and other guests) at a dinner gathering. In the *Gorgias*, Socrates argues that philosophy is an art, whereas rhetoric is a skill based on mere experience.

[4] The poet here refers to Sophocles. This quote is originally from one of his earliest surviving tragedies *Ajax*.

but this is not equally the glory of man. The child is imperfect, and therefore obviously his virtue is not relative to himself alone, but to the perfect man and to his teacher, and in like manner the virtue of the slave is relative to a master.

COMPREHENSION & EXERCISES

Ⅰ. **Read the excerpts from *The Book of Filial Piety* and describe how Xiao (filial piety) is interpreted differently in the following context.**

To oneself

To parents

To elder brothers

To one's ancestors

To one's superiors

Ⅱ. **Read Part II from Aristotle's *Politics* (Book I) and decide whether the following statements are true or false.**

1. Aristotle's main notion is that the ancient Greek polis or city-state is the natural end of human beings.

2. Aristotle believes that only beast and gods have no need for the state.

3. According to Aristotle, the city forms the root of human relationships, but the family is the flower.

4. Aristotle argues that every family is ruled by both man and woman equally.

5. The state is by nature prior to the family and to the individual.

Ⅲ. **Discuss the following questions.**

1. In Chapter XII of *The Book of Filial Piety*, it includes four aspects of filial piety, what are they and why do you think these four aspects are important?

2. According to Confucianism, how can being filial help an individual to leave a good name to later generations?

3. *The Book of Filial Piety*, as a book of traditional Chinese thought of ethics, is the very first one that related filial piety one's parents to loyalty to the sovereign. Explain in your own words the relationship between "loyalty" and "filial piety".

4. In Aristotle's *Politics*, he justified the natural rule of the male over the female. Highlight some examples in the above excerpts from *Politics* (Book I) and try to analyze why Aristotle gracefully excluded women from the political framework of the state.

5. Both Confucius and Aristotle explained the structure of certain kinds of state in terms of the structure of the family. Confucius believed the child should be subordinate to the parent, younger brother to the older, and subject to the sovereign who is to be regarded as the father of the nation. While Aristotle argued that the government of a household is a monarchy, since every house is governed by a single ruler. He also said that husbands exercise a republican government over their wives and monarchical government over their children. Compare and contrast the concept of "family" in *The Book of Filial Piety* and *Politics*.

Session Three (Extensive Reading)
Ten Lectures on Cognitive Linguistics[①]

George Lakoff[②]

I remembered an old paper that one of my students has written about metaphor. And the metaphor was that the nation is a family. After you understand larger social groups in terms of smaller social groups, especially family and communities and so on. This We speak of our founding fathers. When we have a war, we send our sons and daughters off to fight. The nation is understood, at least in America, as a family. This may well be true in China as well.

But Americans conceive of two different models of the family. These in turn lead to two different understandings of the nation. I'll claim two different models of the family. I'll call them the strict-father family and nurturant-parent family. The strict-father family goes with conservatism and the nurturant-parent family goes with liberalism.

The Strict-Father Family

In a strict-father family, the father is the leader of the family. It is assumed that the world is a difficult, competitive, and dangerous place. And it always will be. There is evil out there in the world, and the children are born bad and have to be made good. You need a strict father to protect the family, to support the family, to compete with other people in the world successfully, and to teach the children right from wrong. It is assumed that the strict father knows absolutely what's right and what's wrong. The strict father teaches children what's right by punishing them when they do wrong. The punishment must be painful—it must hurt. It is called physical discipline. If you give them physical discipline when they're young, then they will get mental discipline, they will learn to do what's right and avoid what's wrong. They will control themselves, discipline themselves and that's the only way they become moral people. So physical punishment is an act of love, and there's a name for this "tough love."

---

①This excerpt is adapted from George Lakoff's *Ten Lectures on Cognitive Linguistics* (*Lecture* 5 *Constructions: The Structure of Grammar*). The whole lecture is transcribed from the audio recordings by editors from Beihang University. This lecture is among the keynote lectures series: *Distinguished lectures in Cognitive Linguistics*.

②George Philip Lakoff (1941 -) is an American cognitive linguist and philosopher. He has served as a professor of Linguistics at the University California at Berkeley since 1972 and he is best known for his thesis that people's lives are significantly influenced by the conceptual metaphors they use to explain complex phenomena.

Self-discipline promises still more. If you're a disciplined person, and you pursue your self-interest, you can become wealthy and self-reliant. There is a connection between prosperity and morality. If you are disciplined enough, the assumption is that in America there is so much opportunity you can make money, that all you need is to be disciplined to do it and then you will be able to become self-reliant and make enough money to take care of yourself. If you are not disciplined, then you won't be able to make a living and you will be dependent on other people. Lack of discipline thus seems linked to poverty and immorality, just as there is a link between morality and prosperity.

By the time the child has reached the age of 18 to 21, then the effect of the strict father is over and presumably the children can take care of themselves or not. They have to go off on their own, and if they cannot take care of themselves, too bad. They are subject to the discipline of the world. That's tough love. After that, the father cannot meddle the life of the child. But if the child is on his own and has his own sense of morality and has it right, he doesn't need to be told by the father, so the father is just meddling in his life. Otherwise, the father can't do much good anyway. So the father shouldn't meddle in the life of the child. That's strict-father model.

This model has a metaphorical version of capitalism built into it. It's a fundamental metaphor of capitalism that goes like this. If everybody pursues their own profit, if everybody tries to make as much money they can, then the profit of everybody will be maximized as a law of nature. That is Adam Smith's law of the invisible hand.

Now according to the strict-father model applied to politics, social programs to help the poor, the sick or the aged, are immoral because they give people things they have not earned and that makes them dependent. They take away discipline and that makes them immoral. So the goal of conservative politics is to diminish or even to get rid of government social programs.

The Nurturant-Parent Family

The nurturant-parent family is a very different kind of family. It assumes children are born good and should be made better. And it assumes that the world can be made better and people should act to make the world better. Also it assumes both parents are equal, that they have equal responsibility. The job of these parents is to nurture their children and to raise their children to nurture others. Nurturance means two things: empathy and responsibility. When you ha empathy, you care about someone else, you feel what other people feel, you connect to them, so a parent has to hear the cries of a child and know what those cries mean. Responsibility requires attention to larger issues. Parents cannot be responsible if they cannot take care of themselves. They have to take care of themselves and also take care of their children. To be responsible you have to be strong. It's not easy to raise a child. It requires responsibility. From empathy and responsibility, many things follow. First, you empathize with the child. You want to protect the child, so protection is a moral value. You are morally obligated to protect the child. Second, fulfillment in life is a concern. In America, you want your children to have a happy, fulfilled life, and if you're going to do that, you yourself should have a happy, fulfilled life, because people who are unhappy don't want other people to be happier than they are. So it is part of the nurturant-parent family that everybody in the family should have happy fulfilled lives.

Next, if you empathize with someone, a child, you want the child to be treated fairly. So fairness becomes a value. If you want the child to have a fulfilled life, the child must have freedom to do so. So freedom becomes a value. But there is not much freedom if there is no opportunity to make a living. So allowing opportunity for as many people as possible becomes a value. There is no opportunity if you don't have any prosperity. So building prosperity, living in a good economy for everyone to prosper, no matter who they are, becomes a value. You can't do that unless you build community, unless people are cooperating, so building communities and cooperation are values, values which depend on mutual trust. You don't trust someone unless they're honest. So honesty becomes a value. And you don't trust people unless you can communicate with them. And if you can talk back and forth, open communication is a value. These values go to make up a liberal idea of capitalism.

So you have two completely opposite views of politics in America that come out from these metaphors of the family. These metaphors run deep. They are usually unconscious. These deep metaphors structure attitudes in every area of life, for education, how you should conduct a foreign policy, how you should run an economy, for every other policy.

There are lots of other metaphor that goes with this. For example, there is a metaphor for what I call free markets. It says a market is a force of nature. And under nature, people should just freely sell goods as best they can. That's a conservative metaphor that fits the strict-father model. It doesn't fit the nurturant-parent model because the market can hurt people. It isn't fair because what happens in the free market is that, the richer you are, the more you can control the market, and then you don't have a fair market. So liberals want fair markets in which wealthy corporations are limited in their abilities to control the market. And conservatives want free markets allowing rich people to get as rich as they can be, because being wealthy is like being a good person.

For example, tax relief is a metaphor and it's a kind of surface metaphor, but the deep metaphor that governs all of the surface metaphors. So the point of all this is that politics and morality can be governed by deep metaphors that determine how you understand the world. The reason why liberals and conservatives in American politics cannot understand each other is that they talk past each other because they are loyal to two utterly different deep metaphors.

Unit Nine Travel

五岳归来不看山,黄山归来不看岳。

——徐霞客(明朝地理学家、游记作家)

　　Having seen the Five Great Mountains, one does not see other mountains; having seen Huangshan, one does not see the Five Great Mountains
　　　　—Xu Xiake(Chinese travel writer and geographer of the Ming dynasty)

　　Scotland is the country above all others that I have seen, in which a man of imagination may carve out his own pleasures; there are so many inhabited solitudes.
　　　　　　　　—Dorothy Wordsworth(English author, poet and diarist)

Session One
Terrace of Heaven Mountain (Tiantaishan You Ji)

Xu Xiake

ABOUT THE AUTHOR

Xu Xiake has been canonized as the ultimate Chinese traveler. He possessed a rare commitment to an unencumbered life devoted exclusively to traveling, and produced monumental diaries that dwarf all other efforts. Xu was born in Jiangyin, in present-day Jiangsu Province, into an old scholar family that had fled south after the fall of the Northern Sung. His immediate forebears were of some literary reputation who declined to enter the government during the turbulent politics of the late Ming, preferring to lead leisurely, comfortable lives as local gentry on their estates. His father, Xu Youmian, about whom the connoisseur Chen Jiru (1558A.D.-1639A.D.) wrote a biography, enjoyed traveling to nearby scenic places. He died in 1604 from wounds inflicted by marauding bandits near his home.

After a youth in which he pored over books on geography, travel, history, and Taoism, Xu Xiake decided at the age of twenty-two to devote his life exclusively to visiting the places he had read about; he never even bothered to take the official examinations. Rather, for thirty-three years until his death at the age of fifty-five he traveled to more than sixteen of the modern provinces, often venturing on foot and facing robbers, desertion of servants, the death of companions, lack of food and shelter, inclement weather, and illness. In between journeys, he returned home for brief periods, during which he married twice, raised a family, and was particularly devoted to his mother. Indeed, she was extraordinary for encouraging his unconventional ambitions and even accompanied him on one of his shorter journeys at the age of eighty. With her death in 1625, Xu felt free to roam more widely his most strenuous travels thus took place in his later years.

Although Xu saw himself in the tradition of epic figures such as Xuan Zang[①] and Yeh-lü Ch'u-ts'ai[②], he differed from them in the purity of his motivation. He traveled neither for

---

[①] Xuan Zang (602A.D.-664A.D.) was a 7th-century Chinese Buddhist monk, scholar, traveller, and translator. He is known for the epoch-making contributions to Chinese Buddhism, the travelogue of his journey to India in 629A.D.-645A.D., his efforts to bring over 657 Indian texts to China, and his translations of some of these texts.

[②] Yeh-lü Ch'u-ts'ai (1189A.D.-1243A.D.) was an administrator for Genghis Khan. He assumed that post in 1218 and accompanied Genghis as adviser, astrologer and secretary. He filled similar role for Ögedei, the emperor after Genghis's death in 1227. Yeh-lü organized conquered territories under a central government, which was a monumental task. He set taxes, formed a bureaucracy, controlled regional military leaders, and completed a census.

religious merit nor out of political necessity but in the idealistic spirit of Taoist "free and easy wandering" as well as an insatiable curiosity about the natural world. Initially, he was attracted by scenic beauty and the aura of these places in the literary tradition. In his later journeys, he became more interested in geographical questions, and a number of his hypotheses about such features as cave formations have since been validated by modern scientists. Xu enjoyed a wide range of acquaintances, including many prominent scholars, who regarded him as something of a legend. They valued highly the hand-copied sections of his travel diary that they were able to read.

Xu's s diary was compiled over the course of his travels. He would write at the end of each day, if possible, or several days later, relying on his excellent memory to preserve the details of what he had seen. His entries ranged from about 250 characters to over 4,000. Although some diaries were lost, those that were preserved cover a period from 1613 to 1639 and amount to over 600,000 characters. The diaries were basically notes that Xu kept on the road for his own benefit. Unlike other travel writing, they were not polished literary pieces intended for publication in their original form. He did in fact plan to publish them eventually, but he died unexpectedly from an illness contracted on the road and was unable to edit them. At first, therefore, they were hand-copied by his friend Ji Mengliang in 1642. Subsequently, one of his sons recovered more diaries, printing them in a 1684 edition that is no longer extant. In 1776, Xu's grandson published another corrected edition. Further printings throughout the nineteenth and twentieth centuries popularized the diaries.

The literary appeal of the diaries lies in their spontaneous, unfinished form. Lacking a commemorative occasion or a moralistic intent, they present a relatively objective, unmediated vision of the world in the tradition of "the classification of things." Xu's narration of his journey, which is recorded with meticulous detail in a concise prose style, conveys the experience of a direct encounter with the landscape. Though his diaries do not project a strong sense of personality, they capture the reality of travel more than other writers had, even to the point of noting the food consumed and the condition of his lodgings. Xu's prose is rich in figurative expressions, and his descriptions include visionary perceptions of Nature as an ever-fascinating texture of interacting phenomena. He incorporates lyric responses to the environment in short, poetic phrases. Occasionally, there are subjective opinions and even moments of humor. The sheer magnitude of his diaries and their accuracy have earned them considerable documentary credibility. Whether retracing his footsteps or engaging in "recumbent traveling," readers have considered his diaries to be the ultimate example of aesthetic realism in Chinese travel writing.

ABOUT THE "TERRACE OF HEAVEN MOUNTAIN"

"Terrace of Heaven Mountain" is located in the north of modern Tiantai, Zhejiang

Province. Though not especially difficult to climb, it was originally considered remote and mysterious. Sun Chuo① (314A.D. - 371A.D.), a member of Wang Xizhi's② circle, was among the first to celebrate it in his imaginary "Rhapsody on a Journey to Terrace of Heaven Mountain"③. The Taoist alchemist Ge Hong④ (284A.D. - 362A.D.) also praised it as a suitable place for manufacturing elixirs. But it was largely developed as a spiritual site by Buddhists   indeed, it was the place of origin of the Tiantai school⑤, founded by the monk Zhiyi⑥ (530A.D. - 597A.D.), which later spread to Japan. In his twenty-three years on the mountain, Zhiyi built twelve temples. The major one was the Temple of the Peaceful Nation, which Zhiyi dreamed would bring tranquility to the country. It was completed in 598. Later, in the eighth century, the temple was home to the three reclusive monks Fenggan, Hanshan, and Shide. It had been lavishly restored twelve years before Xu's visit.

The mountain is actually a range that extends from Transcendent's Mist Mountain (Hsien-hsia-shan) northward to the Chou-shan Archipelago. Its highest point, 3,732-foot Lotus Summit (Hua-tingshan), is encircled by lesser peaks. The mountain contains eight famous scenes, of which the arched Rock Bridge (Shi-liang) is the most notable, extending twenty-three feet across a waterfall 140 feet high; its narrowest section is only one-half foot wide. The following selection records Xu Xiake's first visit to the mountain together with the monk Lien-chou; he returned for another visit in 1632A.D..

---

①Sun Chuo was a Chinese poet of the Six Dynasties poetry tradition. He was one of the famous participants of the Orchid Pavilion Gathering, along with Wang Xizhi, and a large group of other scholar-poets, in 353A.D., in Shan-yin (now part of the modern province of Zhejiang). Sun Chuo is also famous for a fu upon the topic of Mount Tiantai, as well as his pioneering work on Chinese landscape poetry.

②Wang Xizhi (303A.D. - 361A.D.) was a Chinese calligrapher, politician, general and writer during the Jin dynasty. He was best known for his mastery of Chinese calligraphy. Wang is sometimes regarded as the greatest Chinese calligrapher in Chinese history, and was a master of all forms of Chinese calligraphy, especially the running script. Furthermore, he is known as one of the Four Talented Calligraphers (四贤) in Chinese calligraphy. Emperor Taizong of Tang admired his works so much that the original Preface to the Poems Composed at the Orchid Pavilion (or Lanting Xu) was said to be buried with the emperor in his mausoleum.

③《游天台山赋》.

④Ge Hong was a Chinese linguist, philosopher, physician, politician, and writer during the Eastern Jin Dynasty. He was the author of *Essays on Chinese Characters, the Baopuzi*, among others. He is the originator of First Aid in Traditional Chinese Medicine and influenced later generations.

⑤The name of the school is derived from the fact that Zhiyi lived on Tiantai Mountain, which then became a major center for the tradition. Zhiyi is also regarded as the first major figure to form an indigenous Chinese Buddhist system. Tiantai is sometimes also called "The Lotus School", after the central role of the Lotus Sutra in its teachings.

⑥Zhiyi is the fourth patriarch of the Tiantai tradition of Buddhism in China. He is famous for being the first in the history of Chinese Buddhism to elaborate a complete, critical and systematic classification of the Buddhist teachings. He is also regarded as the first major figure to make a significant break from the Indian tradition, to form an indigenous Chinese system.

READING

游天台山日记

徐霞客

癸丑之三月晦①,自宁海出西门。云散日朗,人意山光,俱有喜态。三十里,至梁隍山②。闻此於菟夹道,月伤数十人③,遂止宿焉。

四月初一日早雨。行十五里,路有岐,马首西向台山,天色渐霁。又十里,抵松门岭,山峻路滑,舍骑步行。自奉化来,虽越岭数重,皆循山麓;至此迂回临陟,俱在山脊④。而雨后新霁,泉声山色,往复创变⑤,翠丛中山鹃映发,令人攀历忘苦。又十五里,饭于筋竹庵。山顶随处种麦。从筋竹岭南行,则向国清大路。适有国清僧云峰同饭,言此抵石梁,山险路长,行李不便,不若以轻装往,而重担向国清相待。⑥余然之。令担夫随云峰往国清,余与莲舟上人就石梁道。行五里,过筋竹岭。岭旁多短松,老干屈曲,根叶苍秀,俱吾阊门盆中物也⑦。又三十余里,抵弥陀庵。上下高岭,深山荒寂,恐藏虎,故草木俱焚去。泉轰风动,路绝旅人⑧。庵在万山坳中,路荒且长,适当其半,可饭可宿。

初二日,饭后,雨始止。遂越潦攀岭,溪石渐幽,二十里,暮抵天封寺。卧念晨上峰顶,以朗霁为缘⑨,盖连日晚霁,并无晓晴。及五更梦中,闻明星满天,喜不成寐。⑩

初三日,晨起,果日光烨烨,决策向顶。上数里,至华顶庵;又三里,将近顶,为太白堂,俱无可观。闻堂左下有黄经洞,乃从小径。二里,俯见一突石,颇觉秀蔚。至则一发僧结庵于前,恐

---

①"癸丑之三月晦": the last day of the third month in the year gui-chou.

②"梁隍山": Guardian Liang's Mountain was named after a prince of the Liang dynasty who fled there during a civil war.

③"闻此於菟即老虎夹道,月伤数十人": I heard that tigers were stalking the roads hereabout and had injured several tens of people in a month.

④"至此迂回临陟,俱在山脊": Now the road began to wind around as we ascended along the spine of the mountain.

⑤"雨后新霁,泉声山色,往复创变": It had cleared after the rain so that the sound of springs and the colors of the mountains were transformed all over.

⑥"不若以轻装往,而重担向国清相待": He suggested I travel lightly and have the heavier things brought to the temple to await me.

⑦"老干屈曲,根叶苍秀,俱吾阊门盆中物也": Their old trunks are bent and twisted with beautiful blue-green needles—just right for the kind of potted trees one sees in Su-chou.

⑧"泉轰风动,路绝旅人": Cascades thundered, and the wind gusted; there were no travelers along this lonely stretch.

⑨"卧念晨上峰顶,以朗霁为缘": As I lay in bed, I wondered about the ascent to the summit the next morning and hoped that clear weather would be an auspicious sign.

⑩"及五更梦中,闻明星满天,喜不成寐": As I lay dreaming during the fifth watch [3:00 – 5:00 A.M.], I heard a voice say that there were bright stars filling the sky and was so happy I could not go back to sleep.

风自洞来,以石瓮塞其门,大为叹惋。复上至太白,循路登绝顶。荒草靡靡,山高风冽,草上结霜高寸许,而四山回映,琪花玉树,玲珑弥望①。岭角山花盛开,顶上反不吐色,盖为高寒所勒耳。

仍下华顶庵,过池边小桥,越三岭。溪回山合,木石森丽,一转一奇,殊惬所望②。二十里,过上方广,至石梁,礼佛昙花亭,不暇细观飞瀑。下至下方广,仰视石梁飞瀑,忽在天际。闻断桥、珠帘尤胜,僧言饭后行犹及往返,遂由仙筏桥向山后。越一岭,沿涧八九里,水瀑从石门泻下,旋转三曲。上层为断桥,两石斜合,水碎迸石间,汇转入潭;中层两石对峙如门,水为门束,势甚怒;下层潭口颇阔,泻处如阈,水从坳中斜下。三级俱高数丈,各级神奇,但循级而下,宛转处为曲所遮,不能一望尽收,又里许,为珠帘水,水倾下处甚平阔,其势散缓,滔滔汩汩。余赤足跳草莽中,揉木缘崖意指攀住树枝爬上高岩,莲舟不能从。暝色夜色四下,始返。停足仙筏桥,观石梁卧虹,飞瀑喷雪,几不欲卧③。

初四日,天山一碧如黛④。不暇晨餐,即循仙筏上昙花亭,石梁即在亭外。梁阔尺余,长三丈,架两山坳间。两飞瀑从亭左来,至桥乃合流下坠,雷轰河颓,百丈不止。余从梁上行,下瞰深潭,毛骨俱悚。梁尽,即为大石所隔,不能达前山,乃还。过昙花,入上方广寺。循寺前溪,复至隔山大石上,坐观石梁。为下寺僧促饭,乃去。饭后,十五里,抵万年寺,登藏经阁。阁两重,有南北经两藏。寺前后多古杉,悉三人围,鹤巢于上,传声嘹呖而清远,亦山中一清响也⑤。是日,余欲向桐柏宫,觅琼台、双阙,路多迷津,遂谋向国清。国清去万年四十里,中过龙王堂。每下一岭,余谓已在平地,及下数重,势犹未止,始悟华顶之高,去天非远! 日暮,入国清,与云峰相见,如遇故知,与商探奇次第⑥。云峰言:"名胜无如两岩,虽远,可以骑行。先两岩而后步至桃源,抵桐柏,则翠城、赤城,可一览收矣。"

初五日,有雨色,不顾,取寒、明两岩道,由寺向西门觅骑。骑至,雨亦至。五十里至步头,雨止,骑去。二里,入山,峰萦水映,木秀石奇,意甚乐之⑦。一溪从东阳来,势甚急,大若曹

---

①"四山回映,琪花玉树,玲珑弥望":jadelike flowers and trees glistened on the mountainsides, creating an intricate splendor wherever I looked.

②"溪回山合,木石森丽,一转一奇,殊惬所望":A stream wound about as the mountains enclosed a scene where the trees and rocks were magnificent and beautiful. Every turn produced some unique sight, satisfying all my expectations.

③"停足仙筏桥,观石梁卧虹,飞瀑喷雪,几不欲卧":Rested at the Bridge of the Transcendent's Raft. Gazed at the Rock Bridge, shaped like a rainbow over the waterfall, which spat out snow-flakes. I almost lost all desire to go to sleep.

④"天山一碧如黛":The sky and the mountain were a single shade of blue-green like mascara.

⑤"传声嘹呖而清远,亦山中一清响也":Their cries reverberated, yet another ethereal sound in these mountains.

⑥"与云峰相见,如遇故知,与商探奇次第":Was met by Yün-feng, and it seemed like encountering an old friend. Discussed with him the marvelous sights I planned to visit.

⑦"峰萦水映,木秀石奇,意甚乐之":The trees were flourishing, and the rocks, extraordinary—I took great pleasure in the scene.

娥①。四顾无筏,负奴背而涉。深过于膝,移渡一涧,几一时。三里,至明岩。明岩为寒山②、拾得③隐身地,两山回曲,《志》所谓八寸关也。入关,则四周峭壁如城。最后,洞深数丈,广容数百人。洞外,左有两岩,皆在半壁;右有石笋突耸,上齐石壁,相去一线,青松紫蕊,翁苁于上,恰与左岩相对,可称奇绝④。出八寸关,复上一岩,亦左向。来时仰望如一隙,及登其上,明敞容数百人。岩中一井。曰仙人井,浅而不可竭。岩外一特石,高数丈,上岐立如两人,僧指为寒山、拾得云。入寺。饭后云阴溃散,新月在天,人在回崖顶上,对之清光溢壁。

初六日,凌晨出寺,六七里至寒岩。石壁直上如劈,仰视空中,洞穴甚多。岩半有一洞,阔八十步,深百余步,平展明朗。循岩石行,从石隘仰登。岩坳有两石对耸,下分上连,为鹊桥,亦可与方广石梁争奇,但少飞瀑直下耳。还饭僧舍,觅筏渡一溪。循溪行山下,一带峭壁巉崖,草木盘垂其上,内多海棠、紫荆,映荫溪色,香风来处,玉兰芳草,处处不绝。已至一山嘴,石壁直竖涧底,涧深流驶,旁无余地。壁上凿孔以行,孔中仅容半趾,逼身而过,神魄为动,自寒岩十五里至步头,从小路向桃源。桃源在护国寺旁,寺已废,土人茫无知者。随云峰莽行曲路中,日已堕,竟无宿处,乃复问至坪头潭。潭去步头仅二十里,今从小路,返迂回三十余里宿。信桃源误人也⑤。

初七日,自坪头潭行曲路中三十余里,渡溪入山。又四五里,山口渐夹,有馆曰桃花坞。循深潭而行,潭水澄碧,飞泉自上来注,为鸣玉涧⑥。涧随山转,人随涧行。两旁山皆石骨,攒簇拥峦夹翠,涉目成赏⑦,大抵胜在寒、明两岩间。涧穷路绝,一瀑从山坳泻下,势甚纵横。出饭馆中,循坞东南行,越两岭,寻所谓"琼台"、"双阙",竟无知者。去数里,访知在山顶。与云峰循路攀援,始达其巅。下视峭削环转,一如桃源,而翠壁万丈过之⑧。峰头中断,即为双阙;双阙所夹而环者,即为琼台。台三面绝壁,后转即连双阙。余在对阙,日暮不及复登,然胜风景已一日尽矣。遂下山,从赤城后还国清,凡三十里。

初八日,离国清,从山后五里登赤城。赤城山顶圆壁特起,望之如城,而石色微赤。岩穴为僧舍凌杂,尽掩天趣。所谓玉京洞、金钱池、洗肠井,俱无甚奇。

---

①"一溪从东阳来,势甚急,大若曹娥":A stream flowed from Tung-yang District with a strong current, as wide as the Maiden Ts'ao River.

②"寒山":Hanshan was a Chinese Buddhist and Taoist figure associated with a collection of poems from the Chinese Tang Dynasty in the Taoist and Chan tradition.

③"拾得":Shide was a Tang Dynasty Chinese Buddhist poet at the Guoqing Temple on Mount Tiantai on the East China Sea coast; roughly contemporary with Hanshan and Fenggan, but younger than both of them.

④"青松紫蕊,翁苁于上,恰与左岩相对,可称奇绝":Green pines and purple flowers flourished on top. It complements perfectly the crags to the left—it could certainly be called a marvel.

⑤"信桃源误人也":Now I believe how Peach Spring can cause travelers to lose their way.

⑥"循深潭而行,潭水澄碧,飞泉自上来注,为鸣玉涧":Followed alongside a deep pond. The water was a clear blue-green. A waterfall poured down into it from above. This was the Ringing Jade Torrent.

⑦"攒簇拥峦夹翠,涉目成赏":The mountains on both sides were like skeletons of rock. Patches of emerald foliage grew among the clustered peaks. Everywhere I looked was delightful.

⑧"下视峭削环转,一如桃源,而翠壁万丈过之":Looked down at sheer peaks, which encircled us just like at Peach Spring but these emerald cliffs were loftier by far.

Session Two
Recollections of a Tour Made in Scotland

Dorothy Wordsworth

ABOUT THE AUTHOR

　　Dorothy Wordsworth (1771A.D. - 1855A.D.) was an English prose writer whose Alfoxden Journal 1798 and Grasmere Journals 1800 - 1803 are read today for the imaginative power of their description of nature and for the light they throw on her brother, theRomantic poet William Wordsworth[①].

　　Their mother's death in 1778 separated Dorothy from her brothers, and from 1783 they were without a family home. The sympathy between William and Dorothy was strong; she understood him as no one else could and provided the "quickening influence" he needed. When in 1795 he was lent a house in Dorset, she made a home for him there. At Alfoxden, Somerset, in 1796A.D. - 1798A.D., she enjoyed with Wordsworth and Samuel Taylor Coleridge[②] a companionship of "three persons with one soul." She went with them to Germany (1798A. D. - 1799A.D.), and in December 1799 she and William settled for the first time in a home of their own, Dove Cottage, Grasmere, in the Lake District, remaining there after his marriage (1802) and moving with the family to Rydal Mount in 1813. In 1829 she was dangerously ill and thenceforth was obliged to lead the life of an invalid. Her ill health affected her intellect, and during the last 20 years of her life her mind was clouded.

　　The Alfoxden Journal (of which only the period from January to April 1798 survives) is a record of William's friendship with Coleridge that resulted in their Lyrical Ballads (1798), with which the Romantic movement began. The Grasmere Journals contains material on which William drew for his poetry (notably her description of daffodils in April 1802, which inspired his "I Wandered Lonely as a Cloud"). Her other surviving journals include accounts of her trip to Germany in 1798A.D. - 1799A.D. as well as visits to Scotland (1803) and Switzerland (1820). None of her writings was published in her lifetime.

---

　　①William Wordsworth (1770A.D. - 1850A.D.) was an English Romantic poet who, with Samuel Taylor Coleridge, helped to launch the Romantic Age in English literature with their joint publication *Lyrical Ballads* (1798).

　　②Samuel Taylor Coleridge (1772A.D. - 1834A.D.) was an English poet, literary critic, philosopher, and theologian who, with his friend William Wordsworth, was a founder of the Romantic Movement in England and a member of the Lake Poets. He also shared volumes and collaborated with Charles Lamb, Robert Southey, and Charles Lloyd. He wrote the poems "The Rime of the Ancient Mariner and Kubla Khan", as well as the major prose work *Biographia Literaria*.

ABOUT *RECOLLECTIONS OF A TOUR MADE IN SCOTLAND*

Recollections of a Tour Made in Scotland, 1803 A.D. is a travel memoir by Dorothy Wordsworth about a six-week, 663-mile journey through the Scottish Highlands from August-September 1803 with her brother William Wordsworth and mutual friend Samuel Taylor Coleridge. Some have called it "undoubtedly her masterpiece" and one of the best Scottish travel literature accounts during a period in the late 18th and early 19th centuries. It is often compared as the Romantic counterpart to the better-known Enlightenment-era *A Journey to the Western Islands of Scotland* (1775 A.D.) by Samuel Johnson① written about 27 years earlier. Dorothy wrote Recollections for family and friends and never saw it published in her lifetime.

The three travellers were important authors in the burgeoning Romanticism movement② and thus the trip itinerary③ was in part a literary pilgrimage to the places associated with Scottish figures significant to Romanticists such as Robert Burns④, Ossian⑤, Rob Roy⑥, William Wallace⑦, and contemporary Sir Walter Scott⑧. Dorothy's descriptions and

---

①Samuel Johnson (1709 A.D.-1784 A.D.), often called Dr Johnson, was an English writer who made lasting contributions as a poet, playwright, essayist, moralist, critic, biographer, editor and lexicographer. The Oxford Dictionary of National Biography calls him "arguably the most distinguished man of letters in English history".

②Romanticism was an artistic and intellectual movement which took place in Europe between the late eighteenth and mid-nineteenth centuries. Understood broadly as a break from the guiding principles of the Enlightenment-which established reason as the foundation of all knowledge-the Romantic Movement emphasised the importance of emotional sensitivity and individual subjectivity. For the Romantics, imagination, rather than reason, was the most important creative faculty.

③A plan of a journey, including the route and the places that will be visited.

④Robert Burns (1759 A.D.-1796 A.D.) was a Scottish poet and lyricist. He is widely regarded as the national poet of Scotland and is celebrated worldwide. He is the best known of the poets who have written in the Scots language, although much of his writing is in a "light Scots dialect" of English, accessible to an audience beyond Scotland.

⑤Ossian is the narrator and purported author of a cycle of epic poems published by the Scottish poet James Macpherson, originally as *Fingal* (1761 A.D.) and *Temora* (1763 A.D.), and later combined under the title *The Poems of Ossian*.

⑥Rob Roy (1671 A.D.-1734 A.D.) was a Scottish outlaw, who later became a folk hero.

⑦William Wallace (1270 A.D.-1305 A.D.) was a Scottish knight who became one of the main leaders during the First War of Scottish Independence. Since his death, Wallace has obtained an iconic status far beyond his homeland. He is the protagonist of Blind Harry's 15th-century epic poem *The Wallace* and the subject of literary works by Jane Porter and Sir Walter Scott, and of the Academy Award-winning film *Braveheart*.

⑧Walter Scott (1771 A.D. - 1832 A.D.) was a Scottish historical novelist, poet, playwright and historian. Many of his works remain classics of European and Scottish literature, notably the novels *Ivanhoe*, *Rob Roy*, *Waverley*, *Old Mortality*, *The Heart of Mid-Lothian* and *The Bride of Lammermoor*, and the narrative poems *The Lady of the Lake and Marmion*. He had a major impact on European and American literature.

judgments of the countryside and landscapes were a mixture of her own personal aesthetics and the in-fashion aesthetics of the sublime, beautiful and picturesque—in fact *Recollections* is considered today a classic of picturesque travel writing.

Venturing to Scotland in 1803 was not an easy trip and the thirty-year-old Dorothy would experience much of the rougher nature of Scottish life. Scotland had become depopulated in areas from emigration throughout the 18th century and the remaining rural Scots existed in a preindustrial lifestyle more reminiscent of the Middle Ages than modern times. The roads were poor and dangerous or mere cattle-paths requiring a local guide. Dorothy notes the road quality along each segment from "most excellent", "roughish", to "very bad" to "wretchedly bad". Finding a place to sleep meant finding a public house along the road, which could range from a pleasant inn by English standards, to a dirty and smoky peasants hut with no glass windows nor chimney and a dirt floor. More than once the Wordsworths were refused a room for the night after dark in the rain with miles to the next town; however, this was contrasted by the kindness and generosity of others. Food in 19th century Scotland along the road ranged from boiled fowl and egg on the high end to whey and oat bread on the low end, and none at all in some cases, although "A boiled sheep's head, with the hair singed off" was a true Scottish fare savoured.

Dorothy wrote the journal over a 20-month period starting in September 1803. "I had written it for the sake of Friends who could not be with us at the time". Her friends admired her *Recollections* and it soon began to circulate and talk of publication became inevitable. In 1822 Dorothy put together a more refined version, she had lost the original and it was completed from memory, but a publisher was never located. It would not be until 1874, nearly 20 years after her death in 1855, that it was published for the first time.

READING

William and I parted from Mary on Sunday afternoon, August 14th, 1803; and William, Coleridge, and I left Keswick[①] on Monday morning, the 15th, at twenty minutes after eleven o'clock. The day was very hot; we walked up the hills, and along all the rough road, which made our walking half the day's journey. Travelled under the foot of Carrock, a mountain covered with stones on the lower part; above, it is very rocky, but sheep pasture there; we saw several where there seemed to be no grass to tempt them. Passed the foot of Grisdale and Mosedale, both pastoral valleys, narrow, and soon terminating in the mountains —green, with scattered trees and houses, and each a beautiful stream. At Grisdale our horse backed upon a steep bank where the road was not fenced, just above a pretty mill at the foot of the valley; and we had a second threatening of a disaster in crossing a narrow bridge between the two dales; but this was not the fault of either man or horse. Slept at Mr. Younghusband's public-house, Hesket Newmarket. In the evening walked to

---

① An English market town in the Lake District.

Caldbeck Falls, a delicious spot in which to breathe out a summer's day—limestone rocks, hanging trees, pools, and waterbreaks—caves and caldrons which have been honoured with fairy names, and no doubt continue in the fancy of the neighbourhood to resound with fairy revels.

    Tuesday, August 16th.—Passed Rose Castle upon the Caldew, an ancient building of red stone with sloping gardens, an ivied gateway, velvet lawns, old garden walls, trim flower-borders with stately and luxuriant flowers. We walked up to the house and stood some minutes watching the swallows that flew about restlessly and flung their shadows upon the sun-bright walls of the old building; the shadows glanced and twinkled, interchanged and crossed each other, expanded and shrunk up, appeared and disappeared every instant; as I observed to William and Coleridge, seeming more like living things than the birds themselves. Dined at Carlisle①; the town in a bustle with the assizes②; so many strange faces known in former times and recognised, that it half seemed as if I ought to know them all, and, together with the noise, the fine ladies, etc., they put me into confusion. This day Hatfield③ was condemned. I stood at the door of the gaoler's house, where he was; William entered the house, and Coleridge saw him; I fell into conversation with a debtor, who told me in a dry way that he was "far over-learned," and another man observed to William that we might learn from Hatfield's fate "not to meddle with pen and ink." We gave a shilling to my companion, whom we found out to be a friend of the family, a fellow-sailor with my brother John④ "in Captain Wordsworth's ship." Walked upon the city walls, which are broken down in places and crumbling away, and most disgusting from filth. The city and neighbourhood of Carlisle disappointed me; the banks of the river quite flat, and, though the holms are rich, there is not much beauty in the vale from the want of trees—at least to the eye of a person coming from England, and, I scarcely know how, but to me the holms had not a natural look; there was something townish in their appearance, a dullness in their strong deep green. To Longtown⑤—not very interesting, except from the long views over the flat country; the road rough, chiefly newly mended. Reached Longtown after sunset, a town of brick houses belonging chiefly to the Graham family. Being in the form of a cross

---

    ①Carlisle is a border city and the county town of Cumbria, as well as the administrative centre of the City of Carlisle district in North West England. Carlisle is located 8 miles (13 km) south of the Scottish border.

    ②The former periodical sessions of the superior courts in English counties for trial of civil and criminal cases.

    ③He was condemned to death at Carlisle on August 16, 1803. His atrocious treatment of a beautiful girl, known in the district as "Mary of Buttermere", had drawn more than usual attention to the criminal.

    ④The "Brother John" here alluded to was a sailor. He was about two years and eight months younger than the William Wordsworth. He perished, with nearly all his crew, in the "Earl of Abergavenny", East-Indiaman, which he commanded, and which, owing to the incompetency of a pilot, was in his last outward voyage wrecked on the Shambles of the Bill of Portland on the night of Friday, February 5, 1805.

    ⑤Longtown is a market town in Cumbria, England, just south of the Scottish Border.

and not long, it had been better called Crosstown. There are several shops, and it is not a very small place; but I could not meet with a silver thimble, and bought a halfpenny brass one. Slept at the Graham's Arms, a large inn. Here, as everywhere else, the people seemed utterly insensible of the enormity of Hatfield's offences; the ostler① told William that he was quite a gentleman, paid everyone genteelly, etc. etc. He and 'Mary' had walked together to Gretna Green; a heavy rain came on when they were there; a returned chaise happened to pass, and the driver would have taken them up; but "Mr. Hope's" carriage was to be sent for; he did not choose to accept the chaisedriver's offer.

Wednesday, August 17th.—Left Longtown after breakfast. About half-a-mile from the town a guide-post and two roads, to Edinburgh and Glasgow; we took the left-hand road, to Glasgow. Here saw a specimen of the luxuriance of the heath-plant, as it grows in Scotland; it was in the enclosed plantations—perhaps sheltered by them. These plantations appeared to be not well grown for their age; the trees were stunted②. Afterwards the road, treeless, over a peat-moss common—the Solway Moss; here and there an earth-built hut with its peat stack, a scanty growing willow hedge round the kailgarth③, perhaps the cow pasturing near,—a little lass④ watching it,—the dreary waste cheered by the endless singing of larks.

We enter Scotland by crossing the river Sark; on the Scotch side of the bridge the ground is unenclosed pasturage; it was very green, and scattered over with that yellow flowered plant which we call grunsel; the hills heave and swell prettily enough; cattle feeding; a few corn fields near the river. At the top of the hill opposite is Springfield, a village built by Sir William Maxwell—a dull uniformity in the houses, as is usual when all built at one time, or belonging to one individual, each just big enough for two people to live in, and in which a family, large or small as it may happen, is crammed. There the marriages are performed. Further on, though almost contiguous, is Gretna Green⑤, upon a hill and among trees. This sounds well, but it is a dreary place; the stone houses dirty and miserable, with broken windows. There is a pleasant view from the churchyard over Solway Firth to the Cumberland mountains. Dined at Annan. On our left as we travelled along appeared the Solway Firth⑥ and the mountains beyond, but the near country dreary. Those houses by the roadside which are built of stone are comfortless and dirty; but we peeped into

---

①One who takes care of horses or mules.

②Slowed or stopped abnormally in growth or development.

③A kitchen-garden, a cabbage garth, though often adorned with a profusion of flowers.

④A young woman.

⑤Gretna Green is a parish in the southern council area of Dumfries and Galloway, Scotland, and is situated on the Scottish side of the border between Scotland and England, defined by the small river Sark, which flows into the estuary of the western contiguous Solway Firth.

⑥The Solway Firth is a firth that forms part of the border between England and Scotland, between Cumbria (including the Solway Plain) and Dumfries and Galloway. Firth is a word in the English and Scots languages used to denote various coastal waters in the United Kingdom, predominantly within Scotland.

a clay "biggin" that was very "canny", and I daresay will be as warm as a swallow's nest in winter. The town of Annan made me think of France and Germany; many of the houses large and gloomy, the size of them outrunning the comforts. One thing which was like Germany pleased me: the shopkeepers express their calling① by some device or painting; bread-bakers have biscuits, loaves, cakes painted on their window-shutters; blacksmiths horses' shoes, iron tools, etc. etc.; and so on through all trades.

Reached Dumfries② at about nine o'clock—market-day; met crowds of people on the road, and every one had a smile for us and our car… The inn was a large house, and tolerably comfortable; Mr. Rogers and his sister, whom we had seen at our own cottage at Grasmere a few days before, had arrived there that same afternoon on their way to the Highlands; but we did not see them till the next morning, and only for about a quarter of an hour.

Thursday, August 18th.—Went to the churchyard where Burns③ is buried. A bookseller accompanied us. He showed us the outside of Burns's house, where he had lived the last three years of his life, and where he died. It has a mean appearance, and is in a bye situation, whitewashed; dirty about the doors, as almost all Scotch houses are; flowering plants in the windows.

Went on to visit his grave. He lies at a corner of the churchyard, and his second son, Francis Wallace, beside him. There is no stone to mark the spot④; but a hundred guineas⑤ have been collected, to be expended on some sort of monument. "There," said the bookseller, pointing to a pompous monument, " there lies Mr. Such-a-one"—I have forgotten his name,—"a remarkably clever man; he was an attorney, and hardly ever lost a cause he undertook. Burns made many a lampoon⑥ upon him, and there they rest, as you see." We looked at the grave with melancholy and painful reflections, repeating to each other his own verses:—

"Is there a man whose judgment clear

---

①The vocation or profession in which one customarily engages; business or trade.

②Dumfries is a market town and former royal burgh within the Dumfries and Galloway council area of Scotland.

③Robert Burns(1759 – 1796) was a Scottish poet and lyricist. He is widely regarded as the national poet of Scotland.

④"The body of Burns was not allowed to remain long in this place. To suit the plan of a rather showy mausoleum, his remains were removed into a more commodious spot of the same kirkyard on the 5th July 1815. The coffin was partly dissolved away; but the dark curling locks of the poet were as glossy, and seemed as fresh, as on the day of his death."—*Life of Burns*, by Allan Cunningham.

⑤The Guinea was a coin, minted in Great Britain between 1663 and 1814, that contained approximately one-quarter of an ounce of gold. The name came from the Guinea region in West Africa, from where much of the gold used to make the coins was sourced.

⑥A harsh satire usually directed against an individual.

Can others teach the course to steer,
Yet runs himself life's mad career
Wild as the wave? —
Here let him pause, and through a tear
Survey this grave.
The Poor Inhabitant below
Was quick to learn, and wise to know,
And keenly felt the friendly glow
And softer flame;
But thoughtless follies laid him low,
And stain'd his name."

The churchyard is full of grave-stones and expensive monuments in all sorts of fantastic shapes—obelisk-wise, pillar-wise, etc. In speaking of Gretna Green, I forgot to mention that we visited the churchyard. The church is like a huge house; indeed, so are all the churches, with a steeple, not a square tower or spire, —a sort of thing more like a glass-house chimney than a Church of England steeple; grave-stones in abundance, few verses, yet there were some—no texts. Over the graves of married women the maiden name instead of that of the husband, "spouse" instead of "wife," and the place of abode preceded by "in" instead of "of." When our guide had left us, we turned again to Burns's house. Mrs. Burns was gone to spend some time by the sea-shore with her children. We spoke to the servant-maid at the door, who invited us forward, and we sat down in the parlour. The walls were coloured with a blue wash; on one side of the fire was a mahogany desk, opposite to the window a clock, and over the desk a print from the "Cotter's Saturday Night," which Burns mentions in one of his letters having received as a present. The house was cleanly and neat in the inside, the stairs of stone, scoured white, the kitchen on the right side of the passage, the parlour on the left. In the room above the parlour the Poet died, and his son after him in the same room. The servant told us she had lived five years with Mrs. Burns, who was now in great sorrow for the death of 'Wallace.' She said that Mrs. Burns's youngest son was at Christ's Hospital.

...

COMPREHENSION & EXERCISES

Ⅰ. **Read "Terrace of Heaven Mountain" and explain the italicized parts in English.**

1. I had heard that below to the left of the cottage was the Cave of the Yellow Court Scripture, so we followed a narrow path for less than a mile to where I gazed down upon a rock boldly protruding and found it quite *exquisite* and flourishing.

2. Cranes make their nests on top. Their cries reverberated, yet another *ethereal* sound in these mountains.

3. After a meal, the clouds *dispersed* and the new moon appeared in the sky. I stood on

the summit of this undulating cliff and watched the pure light flood the rock walls.

4. What they surround and enclose is the Jade Terrace. Three sides of the terrace are *precipitous* cliffs, and the rear is connected to the Double Gatetowers.

Ⅱ. **Read "Terrace of Mountain Heaven" and *Recollections* and answer the questions.**

1. In what order do Xu Xiake and Dorothy Wordsworth narrate their travels? Are there any similarities in their style and content?

2. Xu Xiake depicted what he saw in *Terrace of Mountain Heaven* in such vivid details that the scenery seems to be right in front of the reader's eyes. Can you give some examples of his presentation of scenic beauty?

3. Far from being intimidated from the difficulty of mountain climbing, Xu Xiake seems to be zealous about visiting one place of natural/cultural interest after another. How would you describe Xu Xiake as a traveler?

4. Are there any lines in *Terrace of Mountain Heaven* that betray Xu Xiake's flux of emotions?

5. According to Dorothy, what did Rose Castle upon the Caldew look like?

6. Why did Dorothy say "Longtown had better been called Crosstown"?

7. How did Gretna Green strike Dorothy? What kind of impression did it leave on her?

8. What are Dorothy's observations about the gravestones in the churchyard?

Ⅲ. **Translate the following paragraph into Chinese.**

Passed Rose Castle upon the Caldew, an ancient building of red stone with sloping gardens, an ivied gateway, velvet lawns, old garden walls, trim flower-borders with stately and luxuriant flowers. We walked up to the house and stood some minutes watching the swallows that flew about restlessly and flung their shadows upon the sun-bright walls of the old building; the shadows glanced and twinkled, interchanged and crossed each other, expanded and shrunk up, appeared and disappeared every instant; as I observed to William and Coleridge, seeming more like living things than the birds themselves.

Session Three (Extensive Reading)
The Sketch Book of Geoffrey Crayon, Gent

Washington Irving

The Author's Account of Himself

I was always fond of visiting new scenes, and observing strange characters and manners. Even when a mere child I began my travels, and made many tours of discovery into foreign parts and unknown regions of my native city, to the frequent alarm of my parents, and the emolument of the town crier. As I grew into boyhood, I extended the range of my observations. My holiday afternoons were spent in rambles about the surrounding country. I made myself familiar with all its places famous in history or fable. I knew every spot where a murder or robbery had been committed, or a ghost seen. I visited the neighboring villages, and added greatly to my stock of knowledge, by noting their habits and customs, and conversing with their sages and great men. I even journeyed one long summer's day to the summit of the most distant hill, whence I stretched my eye over many a mile of terra incognita, and was astonished to find how vast a globe I inhabited.

This rambling propensity strengthened with my years. Books of voyages and travels became my passion, and in devouring their contents, I neglected the regular exercises of the school. How wistfully would I wander about the pier-heads in fine weather, and watch the parting ships, bound to distant climes; with what longing eyes would I gaze after their lessening sails, and waft myself in imagination to the ends of the earth!

Further reading and thinking, though they brought this vague inclination into more reasonable bounds, only served to make it more decided. I visited various parts of my own country; and had I been merely a lover of fine scenery, I should have felt little desire to seek elsewhere its gratification, for on no country had the charms of nature been more prodigally lavished. Her mighty lakes, her oceans of liquid silver; her mountains, with their bright aerial tints; her valleys, teeming with wild fertility; her tremendous cataracts, thundering in their solitudes; her boundless plains, waving with spontaneous verdure; her broad, deep rivers, rolling in solemn silence to the ocean; her trackless forests, where vegetation puts forth all its magnificence; her skies, kindling with the magic of summer clouds and glorious sunshine;—no, never need an American look beyond his own country for the sublime and beautiful of natural scenery.

But Europe held forth all the charms of storied and poetical association. There were to be seen the masterpieces of art, the refinements of highly cultivated society, the quaint peculiarities of ancient and local custom. My native country was full of youthful promise;

Europe was rich in the accumulated treasures of age. Her very ruins told the history of the times gone by, and every mouldering stone was a chronicle. I longed to wander over the scenes of renowned achievement—to tread, as it were, in the footsteps of antiquity—to loiter about the ruined castle—to meditate on the falling tower—to escape, in short, from the commonplace realities of the present, and lose myself among the shadowy grandeurs of the past.

I had, besides all this, an earnest desire to see the great men of the earth. We have, it is true, our great men in America: not a city but has an ample share of them. I have mingled among them in my time, and been almost withered by the shade into which they cast me; for there is nothing so baleful to a small man as the shade of a great one, particularly the great man of a city. But I was anxious to see the great men of Europe; for I had read in the works of various philosophers, that all animals degenerated in America, and man among the number. A great man of Europe, thought I, must therefore be as superior to a great man of America, as a peak of the Alps to a highland of the Hudson; and in this idea I was confirmed by observing the comparative importance and swelling magnitude of many English travellers among us, who, I was assured, were very little people in their own country. I will visit this land of wonders, thought I, and see the gigantic race from which I am degenerated.

It has been either my good or evil lot to have my roving passion gratified. I have wandered through different countries and witnessed many of the shifting scenes of life. I cannot say that I have studied them with the eye of a philosopher, but rather with the sauntering gaze with which humble lovers of the picturesque stroll from the window of one print-shop to another; caught sometimes by the delineations of beauty, sometimes by the distortions of caricature, and sometimes by the loveliness of landscape. As it is the fashion for modern tourists to travel pencil in hand, and bring home their portfolios filled with sketches, I am disposed to get up a few for the entertainment of my friends. When, however, I look over the hints and memorandums I have taken down for the purpose, my heart almost fails me, at finding how my idle humor has led me astray from the great object studied by every regular traveller who would make a book. I fear I shall give equal disappointment with an unlucky landscape-painter, who had travelled on the Continent, but following the bent of his vagrant inclination, had sketched in nooks, and corners, and by-places. His sketch-book was accordingly crowded with cottages, and landscapes, and obscure ruins; but he had neglected to paint St. Peter's, or the Coliseum, the cascade of Terni, or the bay of Naples, and had not a single glacier or volcano in his whole collection.

Unit Ten Philosophy

道可道,非常道;名可名,非常名。

——老子(中国哲学家、思想家)

The Tao that can be told of
Is not the Absolute Tao;
The Names that can be given
Are not Absolute Names.

——Laozi(Chinese philosopher & thinker)

　　The investigation of the truth is in one way hard, in another easy. An indication of this is found in the fact that no one is able to attain the truth adequately, while, on the other hand, no one fails entirely, but everyone says something true about the nature of all things, and while individually they contribute little or nothing to the truth, by the union of all a considerable amount is amassed.

——Aristotle(ancient Greek philosopher and scientist)

Session One *The Daode Jing*

Laozi

ABOUT THE AUTHOR

    Laozi is the name of a legendary Daoist philosopher, the alternate title of the early Chinese text better known in the West as *The Daode Jing*, and the moniker of a deity in the pantheon of organized "religious Daoism" that arose during the later Han dynasty (25 A.D.- 220 A.D.). Laozi is the pinyin romanization for the Chinese characters which mean "Old Master." Laozi is also known as Lao Dan ("Old Dan") in early Chinese sources. According to legend, Laozi, the ostensible founder of Daoism, became disgusted with iniquities of life in feudal China and decided to leave his home in the state of Zhou for an unfettered life in the wilderness. When he reached the Western Pass (the border between civilized China and the barbarian wilds), a guard petitioned him to record his teachings for the edification of future generations. The elder sage complied, descended from his donkey and proceeded to write the entirety of *The Daode Jing* in one sitting. When finished, and without a backward glance, Laozi departed through the gate, never to be seen again.

    The earliest ascriptions of authorship of *The Daode Jing* to Laozi are in Hanfeizi and the Huainanzi. Over time, Laozi became a principal figure in institutionalized forms of Daoism and he was often associated with the many transformations and incarnations of the dao itself.

    Despite the fact that after his death he became one of the world's two or three bestselling authors, Laozi never actually died. In traditional China, many people believed that this was so because Laozi had possessed the secret of immortality and had evaded death by transforming his body into a non-perishable form, after which, being able to fly, he had moved his home to heavenly realms. Modern scholars believe that the reason Laozi never died is because he never lived. There was never any such person as Laozi.

ABOUT DAODE JING

    The Daode Jing (meaning "The Classic on the Way and its Power or Virtue") is a famous Chinese philosophical text attributed to the authorship of Laozi (Lao Tzu) (6 B.C.), and highly influential in the religion of Daoism (Taoism). Renowned as the second-most widely translated text in the world after the *Holy Bible*, the *Daode Jing*'s influence on Asian thought, literature and art has been substantial. A small text consisting of a mere five thousand words and divided into 81 chapters, it is written in a pithy style (a set of concise, cryptic aphorisms) and often employs ambiguous and paradoxical language to present profound philosophical teachings. As such, it is open to a variety of interpretations and has generated a substantial corpus of commentaries and translations.

Basic ideas of *the Daode Jing*

The Daode Jing is often a vague and inconsistent book and it is sometimes tempting to wonder whether its authors really had any special insight to offer, or whether they just wanted to sound impressive. But the book does in fact articulate ideas of great originality and interest, ideas that have had enormous influence on Asian culture. The following eight points are among those most central to the text:

1. The nature of the Dao.

There exists in some sense an overarching order to the cosmos, beyond the power of words to describe. This order, which the book refers to as the Dao, has governed the cosmos from its beginning and continues to pervade every aspect of existence. It may be understood as a process that may be glimpsed in all aspects of the world that have not been distorted by the control of human beings, for there is something about us that runs counter to the Dao, and that makes human life a problem. Human beings possess some flaw that has made our species alone insensitive to the Dao. Ordinary people are ignorant of this fact; the Dao de jing tries to awaken them to it.

2. Changing perspective.

To understand the nature of human ignorance, it is necessary to undergo a fundamental change in our perspective. To do this, we need to disentangle ourselves from beliefs we live by that have been established through words and experience life directly. Our intellectual lives, permeated with ideas expressed in language, are the chief obstacle to wisdom.

3. Value relativity.

If we were able to escape the beliefs we live by and see human life from the perspective of the Dao, we would understand that we normally view the world through a lens of value judgments—we see things as good or bad, desirable or detestable. The cosmos itself possesses none of these characteristics of value. All values are only human conventions that we project onto the world. Good and bad are non-natural distinctions that we need to discard if we are to see the world as it really is.

4. Nature and spontaneity.

The marks of human experience are value judgments and planned action. The marks of the Dao are freedom from judgment and spontaneity. The processes of the Dao may be most clearly seen in the action of the non-human world, Nature. Trees and flowers, birds and beasts do not follow a code of ethics and act spontaneously from instinctual responses. The order of Nature is an image of the action of the Dao. To grasp the perspective of the Dao, human beings need to discard judgment and act on their spontaneous impulses. *The Daode Jing* celebrates spontaneous action with two complementary terms, "self-so" and "nonstriving". The inhabitants of the Natural world are "self-so", they simply are as they are, without any intention to be so. Human beings live by purposive action, planning and striving. To become Dao-like, we need to return to an animal-like responsiveness to simple instincts, and act without plans or effort. This "wuwei" style of behavior is the most central imperative Daoist texts recommend for us.

5. The distortion of mind and language.

The source of human deviation from the Dao lies in the way that our species has come to use its unique property, the mind (xin). Rather than allow our minds to serve as a responsive mirror of the world, we have used it to develop language and let our thoughts and perceptions be governed by the categories that language creates, such as value judgments. The mind's use of language has created false wisdom, and our commitment to this false wisdom has come to blind us to the world as it really is, and to the Dao that orders it. The person who practices "wuwei" quiets the mind and leaves language behind.

6. Selflessness.

The greatest barriers to discarding language and our value judgments are our urges for things we believe are desirable and our impulse to obtain these things for ourselves. The selfishness of our ordinary lives makes us devote all our energies to a chase for possessions and pleasures, which leaves us no space for the detached tranquility needed to join the harmonious rhythm of Nature and the Dao. The practice of "wuwei" entails a release from pursuits of self-interest and a self-centered standpoint. The line between ourselves as individuals in accord with the Dao and the Dao-governed world at large becomes much less significant for us.

7. The human influence of the sage.

The selfless power of the sage endows him or her with a social prestige that cannot be matched by ordinary people. So magnificent is the presence of the sage that those who come into contact with such a person cannot help but be deeply influenced. As in the case of Confucianism, De (character, virtue, power) has power over other people, who will spontaneously place themselves under the protection of and seek to emulate the sage.

READING

道德经(节选)

老 子

第一章

道可道,非常道①;名可名,非常名②。无名天地之始③,有名万物之母④。故常无,欲以观其妙;常有,欲以观其徼。此两者同出而异名,同谓之玄,玄之又玄,众妙之门。

第二章

天下皆知美之为美,斯恶已⑤。皆知善之为善,斯不善已。有无相生⑥,难易相成,长短相形,高下相倾,音声相和,前后相随。

第三章

不尚贤,使民不争;不贵难得之货,使民不为盗;不见可欲,使心不乱。是以圣人之治,虚其心,实其腹;弱其志,强其骨。常使民无知无欲。使夫智者不敢为也。⑦为无为⑧,则无不治。

第四章

道冲⑨,而用之或不盈。渊兮⑩,似万物之宗。挫其锐,解其纷,和其光,同其尘。⑪ 湛兮,

---

①"非常道": Absolute Dao, the eternal way can be appreciated only by inner reflection and can be lived only by practice.

②Laozi warns us against falling into the trap of language. The eternal way does not belong to anyone or any religion.

③The Nameless is the origin of Heaven and Earth.

④These lines may be punctuated differently to produce different meanings. One rather common way is 无名,天地之始;有名,万物之母. This translates readily into "The Nameless is the beginning of heaven and earth; the named is the mother of all things." (cf. Lin Yu Tang) The alternative way of punctuating, which some translators(such as Gu Zhengkun(1995)) subscribed to, is: 无,名天地之始;有,名万物之母. A direct translation of this would be: "Non-existence is named the beginning of heaven and earth; Existence is named the mother of all things."

⑤There arises (the recognition of) ugliness.

⑥Being and non-being interdepend in growth, or, existence and emptiness are concepts that make sense by comparison.

⑦Empty their minds and fill their bellies, weaken their wills and strengthen their bones. Always render the people free of knowledge and desire. Ensure that the clever do not dare to act.

⑧Laozi's practice is not about getting what we want but relaxing into the way things are. "Wuwei" is how we come into the world and how we grow and change and return. Laozi's philosophy, was originated from the awareness of human sufferings and injustice in society and he want to do good for other human being in search for a better way to run things in the world.

⑨Tao is a hollow vessel.

⑩Fathomless.

⑪Its sharp edges rounded off; its tangles untied; its light tempered; its turmoil submerged.

似或存。吾不知其谁之子，象帝之先。

第五章

天地不仁，以万物为刍狗①；圣人不仁，以百姓为刍狗。天地之间，其犹橐籥②乎？虚而不屈，动而愈出③。多言数穷，不如守中。

第八章

上善若水。水善利万物而不争，处众人之所恶，故几于道。居善地，心善渊，与善仁，言善信，政善治，事善能，动善时。④ 夫唯不争，故无尤。

第十二章

五色令人目盲；五音令人耳聋；五味令人口爽；驰骋田猎⑤，令人心发狂；难得之货，令人行妨。⑥ 是以圣人为腹不为目，故去彼取此。

第十三章

宠辱若惊，贵大患若身。⑦ 何谓宠辱若惊？宠为上，辱为下，得之若惊，失之若惊，是谓宠辱若惊。何谓贵大患若身？吾所以有大患者，为吾有身，及吾无身，吾有何患？⑧ 故贵以身为天下者，可以寄天下；爱以身为天下者，可以托天下。⑨

第二十二章

"曲则全，枉则直，洼则盈，敝则新，少则多，多则惑。"⑩是以圣人抱一为天下式。不自见，故明；不自是，故彰；不自伐，故有功；不自矜，故长。夫唯不争，故天下莫能与之争。⑪ 古之所谓"曲则全"者，岂虚语哉！诚全而归之。

第二十五章

有物混成，先天地生。寂兮寥兮，独立而不改，周行而不殆，可以为天下母。⑫ 吾不知其

---

①It treats the creation like sacrificial straw-dogs.

②great bellows.

③The more it is moved the more it issues forth.

④In his dwelling, (the Sage) loves the (lowly) earth; In his heart, he loves what is profound; In his relations with others, he loves kindness; In his words, he loves sincerity; In government, he loves peace; In business affairs, he loves ability; In his actions, he loves choosing the right time.

⑤Horse-racing, hunting and chasing.

⑥So goods that are difficult to get become hurdles in our life journey.

⑦Favor and disgrace cause one dismay; What we value and what we fear are within our self.

⑧We have fears because we have a self. When we do not regard that self as self, What have we to fear?

⑨Therefore, he who prizes his body as if it were the world can be given charge of the world. He who loves his body as if it were the world can be entrusted with the world.

⑩When something is bent, it is ready to be put straight; When someone is wronged, one is ready to be redressed; When a container is empty, it is ready to be filled; When something gets old, it is ready to be renewed; When you have just a little, you are ready to get more; When you have got a lot, you are ready to be confused.

⑪Because (in-seeking growth) one never need to struggle or to contest with others, one will never need to fear that one's achievements will be contested away by others.

⑫In the beginning, before the formation of heaven and earth, something had already existed amid the confusion. This lonely existence was totally independent of anything else, and it would not change; It only moved in its own way tirelessly. Only it could have been the mother of heaven and earth.

名,字之曰道,强为之名曰大。大曰逝,逝曰远,远曰反。① 故道大,天大,地大,王亦大。域中有四大,而人居其一焉。人法地,地法天,天法道,道法自然。②

第二十七章
善行,无辙迹;善言,无瑕谪;善计,不用筹策;善闭,无关楗而不可开;善结,无绳约而不可解。③

第三十三章
知人者智,自知者明;胜人者有力,自胜者强。知足者富。强行者有志。不失其所者久。死而不亡者寿。④

第四十五章
大成若缺,其用必敝。大盈若冲,其用不穷。大直若屈,大巧若拙,大辨若讷。⑤ 躁胜寒,静胜热,清静为天下正。

第五十八章
其政闷闷,其民淳淳;其政察察,其民缺缺。祸兮福所倚,福兮祸所伏。

第六十章
治大国,若烹小鲜。以道莅天下,其鬼不神。⑥ 非其鬼不神,其神不伤人。非其神不伤人,圣人亦不伤之。夫两不相伤,故德交归焉。

第六十三章
为无为,事无事,味无味。大小多少。抱怨以德。图难于其易,为大于其细;天下难事,必作于易;天下大事,必作于细。是以圣人终不为大,故能成其大。⑦ 夫轻诺必寡信,多易必多难。是以圣人犹难之,故终无难。

第八十一章
信言不美,美言不信。善言不辨,辨言不善。知者不博,博者不知。圣人不积,既以为人,

---

①These lines have been unnecessarily mystified by some translators. One had them translated thus: "The Great is moving forward without stopping, extending to the remotest distance, and then returning to where it was." Another translation reads: "(Great) means passing on, and passing on means going far away, and going far away means returning."

②Man models himself after the Earth; the Earth models itself after Heaven; the Heaven models itself after Tao; Tao models itself after nature.

③Perfect deeds leave no tracks behind it; perfect speech leaves no flaws to find fault with. Those adept in counting do not require counting chips. Those adept in sealing require no door latches, yet what is sealed cannot be opened. Those adept in tying need produce no knots, yet the strings cannot be untied.

④He who knows others is learned. He who knows himself is wide. He who conquers others has power of muscles. He who conquers himself is strong. He who is contented is rich. He who id determined has strength of will. He who does not lose his center endures. He who dies yet (his power) remains has long life.

⑤The greatest accomplishment appears incomplete, yet it can meet the needs of all occasions. The greatest fulfillment appears to be weak and restrained, yet its use is limitless. What is most straight appears to be bent. What is most dexterous appears to be clumsy. The most skilled of debaters use words sparingly.

⑥To govern a great nation is not much different from frying a small fish. To govern a nation according to the Dao, even the demons will not show their influences.

⑦Therefore the Sage by never dealing with great (problems) accomplishes greatness.

己愈有,既以与人,己愈多。① 天之道,利而不害;圣人之道,为而不争。

Session Two *Metaphysics*

Aristotle

ABOUT THE AUTHOR

See Unit 6.

ABOUTMETAPHYSICS

The first major work in the history of philosophy to bear the title *Metaphysics* was the treatise by Aristotle that we have come to know by that name. But Aristotle himself did not use that title or even describe his field of study as *Metaphysics*; the name was evidently coined by the first century C. E. editor who assembled the treatise we know as Aristotle's "Metaphysics" out of various smaller selections of Aristotle's works. The title *Metaphysics*—literally, "after the Physics"—very likely indicated the place the topics discussed therein were intended to occupy in the philosophical curriculum. They were to be studied after the treatises dealing with nature.

Aristotle defines "first philosophy" (the first of the sciences) as the science of being qua being. Being can be said in different classes of predicates: the substance (Socrates is a man), quality (Socrates is ugly), location (Socrates in the agora), etc.. In short, as all categories of which list we are never given. These are the categories to be addressed by the universal science, science of forms, which will be called *Metaphysical* by the editor of Aristotle.

The book is arranged in 14 sections: A, α, B, Γ, Δ, E, Z, H, Θ, I, K, Λ, M and N (That is Big Alpha, Little Alpha, Beta, Gamma, Delta, Epsilon, Zeta, Eta, Theta, Iota, Kappa, Lambda, Mu and Nu). The subject matter ranges from science to philosophy to theology and catalogues many discussions related to these themes.

Aristotle's *Metaphysics* has been enormously influential in shaping Arabic and Latin medieval thought and has remained central to early modern philosophy as well. Over the last sixty years or so, the *Metaphysics* has been rediscovered by metaphysicians in the analytic philosophy tradition as a source of philosophical insights.

---

① The Sage does not set out to accumulate a fortune or merit, yet as he serves the people, he becomes richer; and as he gives to people, he gets more.

READING

Book I①

All men naturally desire knowledge. An indication of this is our esteem for the senses; for apart from their use we esteem them for their own sake, and most of all the sense of sight. Not only with a view to action, but even when no action is contemplated, we prefer sight, generally speaking, to all the other senses. The reason of this is that of all the senses sight best helps us to know things, and reveals many distinctions. ②

Now animals are by nature born with the power of sensation, and from this some acquire the faculty of memory, whereas others do not. Accordingly the former are more intelligent and capable of learning than those which cannot remember. Such as cannot hear sounds (as the bee, and any other similar type of creature) are intelligent, but cannot learn; those only are capable of learning which possess this sense in addition to the faculty of memory.

Thus the other animals live by impressions and memories, and have but a small share of experience; but the human race lives also by art and reasoning. It is from memory that men acquire experience, because the numerous memories of the same thing eventually produce the effect of a single experience. Experience seems very similar to science and art, but actually it is through experience that men acquire science and art; for as Polus rightly says, "experience produces art, but inexperience chance." Art is produced when from many notions of experience a single universal judgement is formed with regard to like objects. To have a judgement that when Callias③ was suffering from this or that disease this or that benefited him, and similarly with Socrates and various other individuals, is a matter of experience; but to judge that it benefits all persons of a certain type, considered as a class, who suffer from this or that disease (e.g. the phlegmatic or bilious④ when suffering from burning fever) is a matter of art.

It would seem that for practical purposes experience is in no way inferior to art; indeed we see men of experience succeeding more than those who have theory without experience.

---

①Book I (A, Alpha, 980A. D. - 993A. D.) is about first causes and principles: (1) Knowledge of sensation is to science. Wisdom (Sophia) is the science of first causes and principles. (2) Wisdom is the universal science, first principles and its end is the Supreme Good. It is born of wonder and has no end other than itself.

②*Metaphysics*, for Aristotle, was the study of nature and ourselves. In this sense he brings metaphysics to this world of sense experience-where we live, learn, know, think, and speak.

③Callias, (flourished 5th century B.C.), diplomat and a notable member of one of the wealthiest families of ancient Athens. Callias is usually credited with negotiating the peace treaty of 450/449 between the Greeks and the Persians—called the Peace of Callias. This treaty officially concluded the long but intermittent Greco-Persian Wars.

④Fever symptoms.

The reason of this is a that experience is knowledge of particulars, but art of universals; and actions and the effects produced are all concerned with the particular. For it is not man that the physician cures, except incidentally, but Callias or Socrates or some other person similarly named, who is incidentally a man as well. So if a man has theory without experience, and knows the universal, but does not know the particular contained in it, he will often fail in his treatment; for it is the particular that must be treated. Nevertheless we consider that knowledge and proficiency belong to art rather than to experience, and we assume that artists are wiser than men of mere experience (which implies that in all cases wisdom depends rather upon knowledge); and this is because the former know the cause①, whereas the latter do not. For the experienced know the fact, but not the wherefore; but the artists know the wherefore and the cause. For the same reason we consider that the master craftsmen in every profession are more estimable and know more and are wiser than the artisans, because they know the reasons of the things which are done; but we think that the artisans, like certain inanimate objects, do things, but without knowing what they are doing (as, for instance, fire burns); only whereas inanimate objects perform all their actions in virtue of a certain natural quality, artisans perform theirs through habit. Thus the master craftsmen are superior in wisdom, not because they can do things, but because they possess a theory and know the causes.

In general the sign of knowledge or ignorance is the ability to teach, and for this reason we hold that art rather than experience is scientific knowledge; for the artists can teach, but the others cannot. Further, we do not consider any of the senses to be Wisdom. They are indeed our chief sources of knowledge about particulars, but they do not tell us the reason for anything, as for example why fire is hot, but only that it is hot.

It is therefore probable that at first the inventor of any art which went further than the ordinary sensations was admired by his fellow-men, not merely because some of his inventions were useful, but as being a wise and superior person. And as more and more arts were discovered, some relating to the necessities and some to the pastimes of life, the

---

①Metaphysics is the part of philosophy that deals with concepts like being, substance, cause and identity. To really oversimplify, we could say it's the study of how things came to be and what caused them. When speaking of Aristotle's metaphysics, lots of sources center on his idea of cause. According to his ancient work, there are four causes behind all the change in the world. (1) Material cause: according to our famous Greek philosopher, the material cause is the actual physical properties or makeup of a thing that is. It's the stuff we can see, touch, taste, and so on. It's a rather simple one to grasp. (2) Formal cause: stated a bit academically, the formal cause is the structure or design of a being. In layman's terms, we can call it the blueprints, or the plan. The formal cause is what makes it one thing rather than another. (3) Efficient cause: this is the thing or agent which actually brings something about. It's not what it's made of or the plan for how to make it. It's the actual force that brings something into being. (4) Final cause: being a bit more abstract, the final cause is the ultimate purpose for being.

inventors of the latter were always considered wiser than those of the former, because their branches of knowledge did not aim at utility. Hence when all the discoveries of this kind were fully developed, the sciences which relate neither to pleasure nor yet to the necessities of life were invented, and first in those places where men had leisure. Thus the mathematical sciences originated in the neighborhood of Egypt, because there the priestly class was allowed leisure.

The difference between art and science and the other kindred mental activities has been stated in the *Ethics*[①]; the reason for our present discussion is that it is generally assumed that what is called wisdom is concerned with the primary causes and principles, so that, as has been already stated, the man of experience is held to be wiser than the mere possessors of any power of sensation, the artist than the man of experience, the master craftsman than the artisan; and the speculative sciences to be more learned than the productive. Thus it is clear that Wisdom is knowledge of certain principles and causes.

Since we are investigating this kind of knowledge, we must consider what these causes and principles are whose knowledge is Wisdom. Perhaps it will be clearer if we take the opinions which we hold about the wise man. We consider first, then, that the wise man knows all things, so far as it is possible, without having knowledge of every one of them individually; next, that the wise man is he who can comprehend difficult things, such as are not easy for human comprehension (for sense-perception, being common to all, is easy, and has nothing to do with Wisdom); and further that in every branch of knowledge a man is wiser in proportion as he is more accurately informed and better able to expound the causes. Again among the sciences we consider that that science which is desirable in itself and for the sake of knowledge is more nearly Wisdom than that which is desirable for its results, and that the superior is more nearly Wisdom than the subsidiary; for the wise man should give orders, not receive them; nor should he obey others, but the less wise should obey him.

Such in kind and in number are the opinions which we hold with regard to Wisdom and the wise. Of the qualities there described the knowledge of everything must necessarily belong to him who in the highest degree possesses knowledge of the universal, because he knows in a sense all the particulars which it comprises. These things, viz. the most universal, are perhaps the hardest for man to grasp, because they are furthest removed from the senses. Again, the most exact of the sciences are those which are most concerned with the first principles; for those which are based on fewer principles are more exact than those which include additional principles; e. g., arithmetic is more exact than geometry. Moreover, the science which investigates causes is more instructive than one which does not,

---

[①] This distinction goes all the way back to Aristotle, when he defined the intellectual virtue of "art" as a "state of capacity to make something, involving a true course of reasoning", whereas "knowledge" or "science" is a "state of capacity to demonstrate".

for it is those who tell us the causes of any particular thing who instruct us. Moreover, knowledge and understanding which are desirable for their own sake are most attainable in the knowledge of that which is most knowable. For the man who desires knowledge for its own sake will most desire the most perfect knowledge, and this is the knowledge of the most knowable, and the things which are most knowable are first principles and causes; for it is through these and from these that other things come to be known, and not these through the particulars which fall under them. And that science is supreme, and superior to the subsidiary, which knows for what end each action is to be done; i. e. the Good in each particular case, and in general the highest Good in the whole of nature.

Thus as a result of all the above considerations the term which we are investigating falls under the same science, which must speculate about first principles and causes; for the Good, i.e. the end, is one of the causes.

That it is not a productive science is clear from a consideration of the first philosophers.① It is through wonder that men now begin and originally began to philosophize; wondering in the first place at obvious perplexities, and then by gradual progression raising questions about the greater matters too, e.g. about the changes of the moon and of the sun, about the stars and about the origin of the universe. Now he who wonders and is perplexed feels that he is ignorant (thus the myth-lover is in a sense a philosopher, since myths are composed of wonders); therefore if it was to escape ignorance that men studied philosophy, it is obvious that they pursued science for the sake of knowledge, and not for any practical utility. The actual course of events bears witness to this; for speculation of this kind began with a view to recreation and pastime, at a time when practically all the necessities of life were already supplied. Clearly then it is for no extrinsic advantage that we seek this knowledge; for just as we call a man independent who exists for himself and not for another, so we call this the only independent science, since it alone exists for itself.②

Most of the earliest philosophers③ conceived only of material principles as underlying all things. That of which all things consist, from which they first come and into which on their

---

①First philosophy is not the only field of inquiry to study beings. Natural science and mathematics also study beings, but in different ways, under different aspects. The natural scientist studies them as things that are subject to the laws of nature, as things that move and undergo change.

②In speaking of beings which depend upon substance for their existence, Aristotle implicitly appeals to a foundational philosophical commitment which appears early in his thought and remains stable throughout his entire philosophical career: his theory of categories.

③Pre-Socratics, group of early Greek philosophers, most of whom were born before Socrates, whose attention to questions about the origin and nature of the physical world has led to their being called cosmologists or naturalists. Among the most significant were the Milesians Thales, Anaximander, and Anaximenes, Xenophanes of Colophon, Parmenides, Heracleitus of Ephesus, Empedocles, Anaxagoras, Democritus, Zeno of Elea, and Pythagoras.

destruction they are ultimately resolved, of which the essence persists although modified by its affections—this, they say, is an element and principle of existing things. Hence they believe that nothing is either generated or destroyed, since this kind of primary entity always persists. Similarly we do not say that Socrates comes into being absolutely when he becomes handsome or cultured, nor that he is destroyed when he loses these qualities; because the substrate, Socrates himself, persists. In the same way nothing else is generated or destroyed; for there is some one entity (or more than one) which always persists and from which all other things are generated. All are not agreed, however, as to the number and character of these principles. Thales[①], the founder of this school of philosophy, says the permanent entity is water (which is why he also propounded that the earth floats on water). Presumably he derived this assumption from seeing that the nutriment of everything is moist, and that heat itself is generated from moisture and depends upon it for its existence (and that from which a thing is generated is always its first principle). He derived his assumption, then, from this; and also from the fact that the seeds of everything have a moist nature, whereas water is the first principle of the nature of moist things.

COMPREHENSION & EXERCISES

Ⅰ. **Read The Daode Jing and try to explain the following terms in English.**

道
言
无为
上善若水
道法自然
圣人之道,为而不争
信言不美,美言不信

Ⅱ. **Translate the following paragraph in *Metaphysics*.**

All men naturally desire knowledge. An indication of this is our esteem for the senses; for apart from their use we esteem them for their own sake, and most of all the sense of sight. Not only with a view to action, but even when no action is contemplated, we prefer sight, generally speaking, to all the other senses. The reason of this is that of all the senses sight best helps us to know things, and reveals many distinctions.

Ⅲ. **Discuss the following questions.**

1. What evidence does Aristotle give for his famous claim that "all men by nature desire to know"?

---

①Thales was the founder of science in Ancient Greece. He established the Milesian School, which passed on his knowledge, most notably to Anaximander and Pythagoras. Greek science and mathematics peaked about 300 years later, in the era of Archimedes.

2. How might he explain instances of human beings seem to lack this desire? How does Aristotle relate "experience" and "art"? What does he mean by these key terms?

3. In what sense is Wisdom (sophia) the principle of the hierarchy?

4. Aristotle mentions four types of causes. Which type do the "first philosophers" investigate?

5. If Dao is a Chinese word that has no adequate translation into English, how can English speakers hope to make sense of it?

6. Some commentators have suggested "Nature" as the English equivalent of Dao, what do you think of this suggestion?

7. What do you think a Taoist would say is the meaning of life?

8. Compare and contrast the understanding of language in *the Daode Jing* and "Metaphysics".

9. Crucial question for Western Philosophy should be "What is the truth?" i.e. how to look before you leap; in contrast, crucial question for Chinese Philosophy "Where is the Way?" i.e. how to leap without looking. Explain this statement with some examples.

Session Three (Extensive Reading)
Is Happiness Still Possible?

Bertrand Russell[1]

So far we have been considering the unhappy man; we now have the pleasanter task of considering the happy man. From the conversation and the books of some of my friends I have been almost led to conclude that happiness in the modern world has become an impossibility. I find, however, that this view tends to be dissipated by introspection, foreign travel, and the conversation of my gardener. The unhappiness of my literary friends I have considered in an earlier chapter; in the present chapter I wish to make a survey of the happy people that I have come across in the course of my life.

Happiness is of two sorts, though, of course, there are intermediate degrees. The two sorts I mean might be distinguished as plain and fancy, or animal and spiritual, or of the heart and of the head. The designation to be chosen among these alternatives depends, of course, upon the thesis to be proved. I am at the moment not concerned to prove any thesis, but merely to describe. Perhaps the simplest way to describe the difference between the two sorts of happiness is to say that one sort is open to any human being, and the other only to those who can read and write. When I was a boy I knew a man bursting with happiness whose business was digging wells. He was of enormous height and of incredible muscles; he could neither read nor write, and when in the year 1885 he got a vote for Parliament, he learned for the first time that such an institution existed. His happiness did not depend upon intellectual sources; it was not based upon belief in natural law, or the perfectibility of the species, or the public ownership of public utilities, or the ultimate triumph of the Seventh Day Adventists, or any of the other creeds which intellectuals consider necessary to their enjoyment of life. It was based upon physical vigour, a sufficiency of work, and the overcoming of not insuperable obstacles in the shape of rock. The happiness of my gardener is of the same species; he wages a perennial war against rabbits, of which he speaks exactly as Scotland Yard speaks of Bolsheviks; he considers them dark, designing and ferocious, and is of the opinion that they can only be met by means of a cunning equal to their own. Like the heroes of Valhalla who spent every day hunting a certain wild boar, which they killed every evening but which miraculously came to life again in the morning, my gardener can slay his enemy one day without any fear that the enemy will have disappeared the next day. Although well over seventy, he works all day and bicycles sixteen hilly miles to and from his

---

[1] Excerpts from Bertrand Russell's *The Conquest of Happiness*. Russell was a British philosopher, logician, essayist and social critic best known for his work in mathematical logic and analytic philosophy.

work, but the fount of joy is inexhaustible, and it is 'they rabbits' that supply it.

But, you will say, these simple delights are not open to superior people like ourselves. What joy can we experience in waging war on such puny creatures as rabbits? The argument, to my mind, is a poor one. A rabbit is very much larger than a yellow-fever bacillus, and yet a superior person can find happiness in making war upon the latter. Pleasures exactly similar to those of my gardener so far as their emotional content is concerned are open to the most highly educated people. The difference made by education is only in regard to the activities by which these pleasures are to be obtained. Pleasures of achievement demand difficulties such that beforehand success seems doubtful although in the end it is usually achieved. This is perhaps the chief reason why a not excessive estimate of one's own powers is a source of happiness. The man who underestimates himself is perpetually being surprised by success, whereas the man who overestimates himself is just as often surprised by failure. The former kind of surprise is pleasant, the latter unpleasant. It is therefore wise to be not unduly conceited, though also not too modest to be enterprising.

Of the more highly educated sections of the community, the happiest in the present day are the men of science. Many of the most eminent of them are emotionally simple, and obtain from their work a satisfaction so profound that they can derive pleasure from eating and even marrying. Artists and literary men consider itde rigueur to be unhappy in their marriages, but men of science quite frequently remain capable of old-fashioned domestic bliss. The reason for this is that the higher parts of their intelligence are wholly absorbed by their work, and are not allowed to intrude into regions where they have no functions to perform. In their work they are happy because in the modern world science is progressive and powerful, and because its importance is not doubted either by themselves or by laymen. They have therefore no necessity for complex emotions, since the simpler emotions meet with no obstacles. Complexity in emotions is like foam in a river. It is produced by obstacles which break the smoothly flowing current. But so long as the vital energies are unimpeded, they produce no ripple on the surface, and their strength is not evident to the unobservant.

All the conditions of happiness are realised in the life of the man of science. He has an activity which utilises his abilities to the full, and he achieves results which appear important not only to himself but to the general public, even when it cannot in the smallest degree understand them. In this he is more fortunate than the artist. When the public cannot understand a picture or a poem, they conclude that it is a bad picture or a bad poem. When they cannot understand the theory of relativity they conclude (rightly) that their education has been insufficient. Consequently Einstein is honoured while the best painters are left to starve in garrets, and Einstein is happy while the painters are unhappy. Very few men can be genuinely happy in a life involving continual self-assertion against the scepticism of the mass of mankind, unless they can shut themselves up in a coterie and forget the cold outer world. The man of science has no need of a coterie, since he is thought well of by everybody except his colleagues. The artist, on the contrary, is in the painful situation of having to choose between being despised and being despicable. If his powers are of the first order, he must incur one or the other of these misfortunes—the former if he uses his powers, the latter if he does not. This has not been the case always and everywhere. There have been times when even good artists, even when they were young, were thought well of. Julius II, though he might ill-treat Michael Angelo, never supposed him incapable of painting pictures. The modern millionaire, though he may shower wealth upon elderly artists after they have lost their powers, never imagines that their work is as important as his own. Perhaps these circumstances have something to do with the fact that artists are on the average less happy than men of science.

It is customary to say that in our machine age there is less room than formerly for the craftsman's joy in skilled work. I am not at all sure that this is true: the skilled workman nowadays works, it is true, at quite different things from those that occupied the attention of the mediaeval guilds, but he is still very important and quite essential in the machine economy. There are those who make scientific instruments and delicate machines, there are designers, there are aëroplane mechanics, chauffeurs, and hosts of others who have a trade in which skill can be developed to almost any extent. The agricultural labourer and the peasant in comparatively primitive communities is not, so far as I have been able to observe, nearly as happy as a chauffeur or an engine-driver. It is true that the work of the peasant who cultivates his own land is varied; he ploughs, he sows, he reaps. But he is at the mercy of the elements, and is very conscious of his dependence, whereas the man who works a modern mechanism is conscious of power, and acquires the sense that man is the master, not the slave, of natural forces. It is true, of course, that work is very uninteresting to the large body of mere machine-minders who repeat some mechanical operation over and over again with the minimum of variation, but the more uninteresting the work becomes, the more possible it is to get it performed by a machine. The ultimate goal of machine production—from which, it is true, we are as yet far removed—is a system in which everything uninteresting is done by machines, and human beings are reserved for the work involving variety and initiative. In such a world the work will be less boring and less depressing than it has been at any time since the introduction of agriculture. In taking to agriculture mankind decided that they would submit to monotony and tedium in order to diminish the risk of starvation. When men obtained their food by hunting, work was a joy, as one can see from the fact that the rich still pursue these ancestral occupations for amusement. But with the introduction of agriculture mankind entered upon a long period of meanness, misery, and madness, from which they are only now being freed by the beneficent operation of the machine. It is all very well for sentimentalists to speak of contact with the soil and the ripe wisdom of Hardy's philosophic peasants, but the one desire of every young man in the countryside is to find work in towns where he can escape from the slavery of wind and weather and the solitude of dark winter evenings into the reliable and human atmosphere of the factory and the cinema. Companionship and cooperation are essential elements in the happiness of the average man, and these are to be obtained in industry far more fully than in agriculture.

Not so very far removed from the devotion to obscure causes is absorption in a hobby. One of the most eminent of living mathematicians divides his time equally between mathematics and stamp-collecting. I imagine that the latter affords consolation at the moments when he can make no progress with the former. The difficulty of proving propositions in the theory of numbers is not the only sorrow that stamp-collecting can cure, nor are stamps the only things that can be collected. Consider what a vast field of ecstasy opens before the imagination when one thinks of old china, snuff-boxes, Roman coins, arrow-heads, and flint implements. It is true that many of us are too "superior" for these simple pleasures. We have all experienced them in boyhood, but have thought them, for some reason, unworthy of a grown man. This is a complete mistake; any pleasure that does no harm to other people is to be valued. For my part, I collect rivers: I derive pleasure from having gone down the Volga and up the Yangtse, and regret very much having never seen the Amazon or the Orinoco. Simple as these emotions are, I am not ashamed of them. Or consider again the passionate joy of the baseball fan: he turns to his newspaper with avidity, and the radio affords him the keenest thrills. I remember meeting for the first time one of the leading literary men of America, a man whom I had supposed from his books to be filled with melancholy. But it so happened that at that moment the most crucial baseball results were coming through on the radio; he forgot me, literature, and all the other sorrows of our sublunary life, and yelled with joy as his favorite achieved victory. Ever since this incident I have been able to read his books without feeling depressed by the misfortunes of his characters.

Fads and hobbies, however, are in many cases, perhaps most, not a source of fundamental happiness, but a means of escape from reality, of forgetting for the moment some pain too difficult to be faced. Fundamental happiness depends more than anything else upon what may be called a friendly interest in persons and things.

A friendly interest in persons is a form of affectionateness, but not the form which is grasping and possessive and seeking always an emphatic response. This latter form is very frequently a source of unhappiness. The kind that makes for happiness is the kind that likes to observe people and finds pleasure in their individual traits, that wishes to afford scope for the interests and pleasures of those with whom it is brought into contact without desiring to acquire power over them or to secure their enthusiastic admiration. The person whose attitude towards others is genuinely of this kind will be a source of happiness and a recipient of reciprocal kindness. His relations with others, whether slight or serious, will satisfy both his interests and his affections; he will not be soured by ingratitude, since he will seldom suffer it and will not notice when he does. The same idiosyncrasies which would get on another man's nerves to the point of exasperation will be to him a source of gentle amusement. He will achieve without effort results which another man, after long struggles, will find to be unattainable. Being happy in himself, he will be a pleasant companion, and this in turn will increase his happiness. But all this must be genuine; it must not spring from an idea of self-sacrifice inspired by a sense of duty. A sense of duty is useful in work, but offensive in personal relations. People wish to be liked, not to be endured with patient resignation. To like many people spontaneously and without effort is perhaps the greatest of all sources of personal happiness.

I spoke also in the last paragraph of what I call a friendly interest in things. This phrase may perhaps seem forced; it may be said that it is impossible to feel friendly to things. Nevertheless, there is something analogous to friendliness in the kind of interest that a geologist takes in rocks, or an archaeologist in ruins, and this interest ought to be an element in our attitude to individuals or societies. It is possible to have an interest in things which is hostile rather than friendly. A man might collect facts concerning the habitats of spiders because he hated spiders and wished to live where they were few. This kind of interest would not afford the same satisfaction as the geologist derives from his rocks. An interest in impersonal things, though perhaps less valuable as an ingredient in everyday happiness than a friendly attitude towards our fellow creatures, is nevertheless very important. The world is vast and our own powers are limited. If all our happiness is bound up entirely in our personal circumstances it is difficult not to demand of life more than it has to give. And to demand too much is the surest way of getting even less than is possible. The man who can forget his worries by means of a genuine interest in, say, the Council of Trent, or the life history of stars, will find that, when he returns from his excursion into the impersonal world, he has acquired a poise and calm which enable him to deal with his worries in the best way, and he will in the meantime have experienced a genuine even if temporary happiness.

The secret of happiness is this: let your interests be as wide as possible, and let your reactions to the things and persons that interest you be as far as possible friendly rather than hostile.

参 考 文 献

[1] 陈成今. 大中华文库:山海经:汉英对照[M]. 王宏,赵峥,译. 长沙:湖南人民出版社,2010.

[2] 罗经国. 古文观止精选:英汉对照[M]. 北京:外语教学与研究出版社,2019.

[3] 王应麟,周兴嗣. 三字经 千字文 孝经:汉英对照[M]. 孟凡君,彭发胜,顾丹柯,注译. 北京:中译出版社,2015.

[4] 梭罗. 瓦尔登湖:英汉对照[M]. 梁栋,译. 南京:译林出版社,2010.

[5] 莎士比亚. 莎士比亚诗集[M]. 辜正坤,曹明伦,译. 北京:外语教学与研究出版社,2016.

[6] 许渊冲. 许渊冲译诗经[M]. 北京:中译出版社,2021.

[7] ARISTOTLE. Metaphysics[M]. ROSS W D,trans. Sioux Falls:NuVision Publications,2009.

[8] ARISTOTLE. Rhetoric[M]. ROBERTS W R,trans. Mineola:Dover Publications,2004.

[9] 费尔罗. 人文传统:一[M]. 北京:外语教学与研究出版社,2014.

[10] 费尔罗. 人文传统:二[M]. 北京:外语教学与研究出版社,2014.

[11] ROUSSEAU J J. EMILE[M]. Auburn:Book Jungle,2008.

[12] ROUSSEAU J J. The Social Contract[M]. London:Penguin,2004.

[13] LIU HSIEH. The Literary Mind and the Carving of Dragons[M]. Hong Kong:The Chinese University of Hong Kong Press,2015.

[14] STRASSBERG R E. Inscribed Landscapes,Travel Writing from Imperial China[M]. Berkeley,CA:University of California Press,1994.

[15] STEPHEN O. Readings in Chinese Literary Thought[M]. Cambridge:Harvard University Asia Center,1996.

[16] 吴楚材,吴调侯. 古文观止[M]. 北京:中华书局,1959.

[17] 徐霞客. 徐霞客游记[M]. 北京:中华书局,2012.